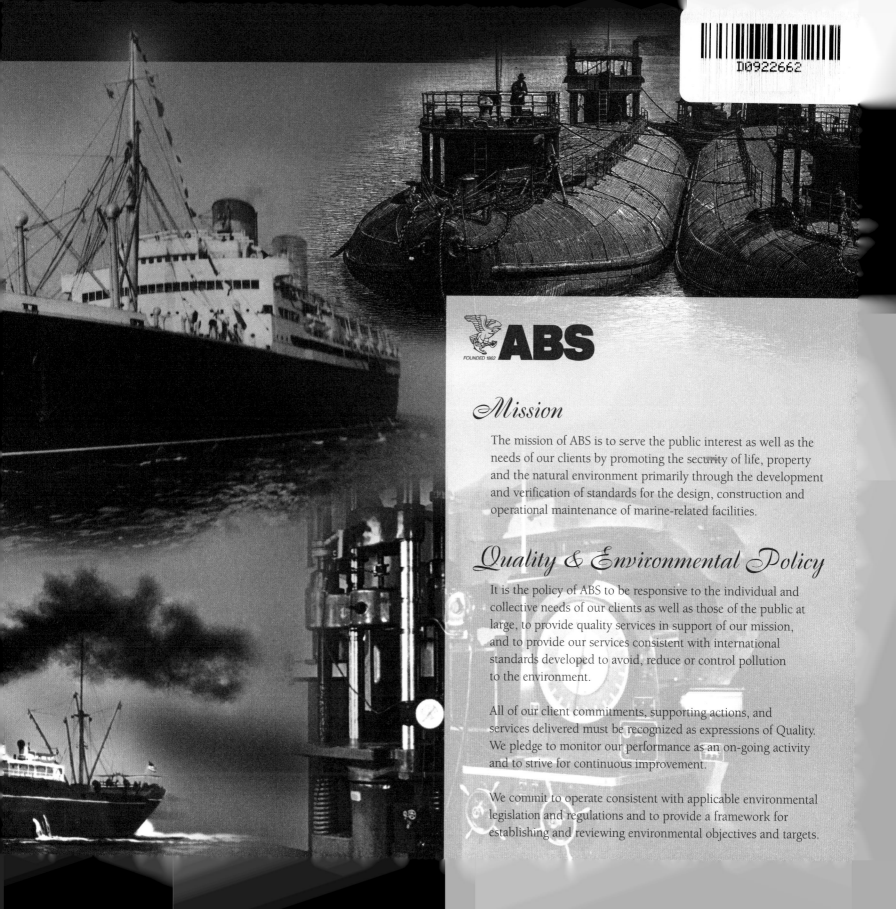

ABS

FOUNDED 1862

Mission

The mission of ABS is to serve the public interest as well as the needs of our clients by promoting the security of life, property and the natural environment primarily through the development and verification of standards for the design, construction and operational maintenance of marine-related facilities.

Quality & Environmental Policy

It is the policy of ABS to be responsive to the individual and collective needs of our clients as well as those of the public at large, to provide quality services in support of our mission, and to provide our services consistent with international standards developed to avoid, reduce or control pollution to the environment.

All of our client commitments, supporting actions, and services delivered must be recognized as expressions of Quality. We pledge to monitor our performance as an on-going activity and to strive for continuous improvement.

We commit to operate consistent with applicable environmental legislation and regulations and to provide a framework for establishing and reviewing environmental objectives and targets.

The *History* of the

AMERICAN BUREAU OF SHIPPING

1862-2005

AMERICAN BUREAU OF SHIPPING

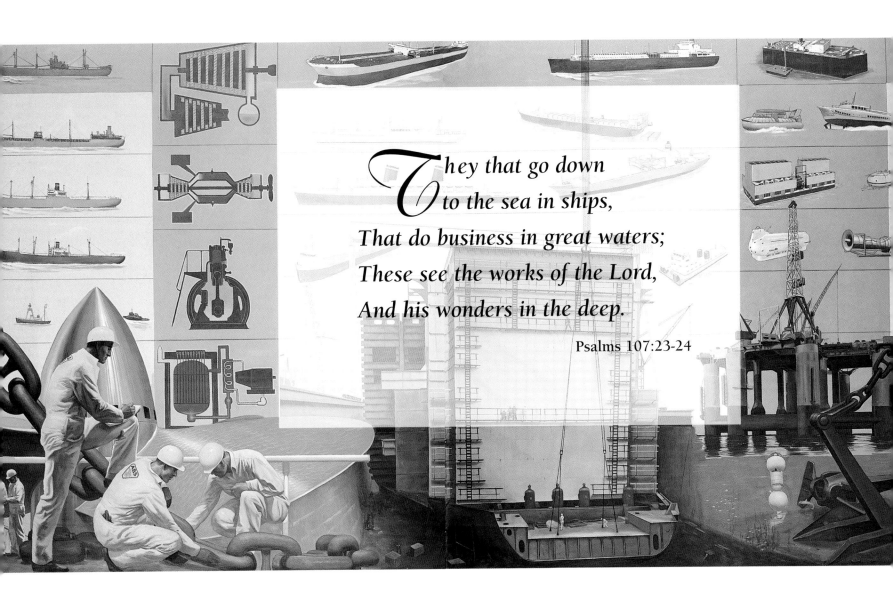

They that go down to the sea in ships,
That do business in great waters;
These see the works of the Lord,
And his wonders in the deep.

Psalms 107:23-24

1862-2005

Sixth Edition

The History of the American Bureau of Shipping
1862-2005

Published by:

ABS
ABS Plaza
16855 Northchase Drive
Houston, TX 77060-6008 USA
Tel: 1-281-877-5800
Fax: 1-281-877-5803
Email: abs-worldhq@eagle.org
www.eagle.org

Produced by:

ABS External Affairs
Houston, TX USA

ISBN 0-943870-03-8

To protect such men and to preserve the property in their care was the primary incentive for the organization, the historical record of which is herein set forth.

75th Anniversary History of American Bureau of Shipping, 1937

PREFACE

From the time of its formation in 1862, promoting safety has been the core mission of the American Bureau of Shipping. Throughout its illustrious history, ABS has provided an essential service to the maritime industry by establishing technical standards for the way ships and other marine structures are designed, constructed, maintained and operated.

Founded as the American Shipmasters' Association, the original guiding principles of the organization were fourfold: to promote the security of life and property on the seas; to provide shipowners, shipbuilders, underwriters and industry with an accurate classification and registry of merchant shipping; to disseminate information; and to establish qualifications for ships' officers.

The name has changed, as have the responsibilities that ABS has assumed within the modern shipping and offshore industries, but the commitment to these basic principles has never wavered.

This account of the history of ABS underscores one of the key elements of the organization's success – its ability to create, implement and adapt to change. While ABS has built and maintained a strong sense of tradition, it has also demonstrated an ability to plan for the future and to implement those plans with the enterprising spirit necessary for continued success.

The history of ABS is one of accomplishment. Future generations can be expected to build on the organization's proud past, to guard its reputation for integrity and impartiality and to continue the pursuit of this unique mission in the years to come. ≋

"Hearts of Oak and Steel"

ABS Private Collection

1862

AMERICAN SHIPMASTERS' ASSOCIATION FORMED

No area of human activity, including maritime commerce and industry, was left untouched by the onrush of technological innovation in the late 19th and early 20th centuries. This is the story of how the American Shipmasters' Association stayed at the forefront of those changes to emerge and stand today as ABS.

It is the story of the transformation of a small organization, founded in the Clipper ship era, into one of the world's foremost marine classification societies, and a world leader in the development and application of science, technology and management system concepts to manage the risk, improve the safety, enhance the quality and minimize the environmental impact of its clients' business activities in a wide range of industries.

The American Shipmasters' Association was organized in 1861 and became a legal corporation in 1862 under the initiative of John Divine Jones, President of Atlantic Mutual Insurance Company. Leaders of eight other marine insurance companies participated in establishing the Association. These were Sun Mutual, Mercantile Mutual, New York Mutual, Union Mutual, Oriental Mutual, Commercial Mutual, Pacific Mutual and the Anchor Insurance Company. Later the Columbia Marine Insurance Company joined the original group.

The founding membership consisted of marine underwriters, shipmasters, shipbuilders, and others prominent in the field of maritime commerce and within the US government.

Each of the founders and participating companies subscribed $700 and agreed to accept assessment for any deficiency in operating expenses in proportion to the premiums received by each. The Association established its headquarters in the Merchants Exchange on Wall Street in New York City. By the end of its fifth year in operation, the Association was entirely self-sufficient, as it remains today.

The main purpose of the organization was promotion of a high degree of efficiency and character among the masters

JOHN DIVINE JONES

A Founder, 1862
President: 1862-1871; 1881-1886

The Merchants Exchange Building at 55 Wall Street, New York City, headquarters of the American Shipmasters' Association in 1862.

and officers of maritime vessels. To that end, tests were developed to determine their knowledge of nautical science and seamanship. Each applicant found qualified was issued a Commission of Competency by the Association.

The first application for such a Commission was received by the as-yet unincorporated Association in September 1861 from Captain Isaiah Pratt. On 22 April 1862, the Association was formally incorporated by an act of the Legislature of the State of New York. During the first year of official operation a total of 1,488 Commission applications were received.

According to its Constitution and By-laws, the American Shipmasters' Association objectives were:

- the collection and dissemination of information upon subjects of marine or commercial interest;

Certificate cites masters and officers for a high degree of efficiency in seamanship.

- the encouragement of worthy and well-qualified commanders, and other ship's officers, and the keeping of a record of their accomplishments;
- the promoting of security of life and property on the seas;
- the provision to shipowners, shipbuilders, underwriters, shippers and all those interested in maritime commerce, of a faithful and accurate classification and registry of mercantile shipping – all with the primary purpose of helping develop the Merchant Marine of the United States.

Originally the Association used its technical expertise to class vessels into five levels of risk, hence the term classification. Today the same term, classification, implies the vessel is structurally sound and mechanically fit to provide for the safety of the lives and cargoes it may carry. To meet the requirements of class, a vessel must comply with a set of standards, or Rules, for design and construction. Periodic surveys are then conducted to determine continued fitness for service. ≋

1867

FIRST RECORD PUBLISHED

Almost immediately the American Shipmasters' Association adopted a system for surveying, rating and registering vessels. This system took the form of a list entitled *Record of American and Foreign Shipping*, first published in March 1867, in pamphlet form and continued thereafter on a monthly basis.

The first bound volume of *The Record*, published in January 1869, contained a list of vessels and their principal particulars. This included such details as type of rigging, number of decks, materials used, types of deck fastenings, number of boilers, ratings of vessels to carry perishable cargoes for a particular duration of voyage, and other facts of interest to underwriters, financial institutions and shippers. The master's name also appeared in *The Record* with his vessel. An asterisk placed by his name indicated he held a Commission with the American Shipmasters' Association.

An early booklet published by the Association contained not only a list of those individuals who had applied for Certificates of Competency, but also practical suggestions for Masters of vessels and the Rules of the Road at Sea. The booklet included the following creed which guided many generations of seafarers under the title "The Seaman's Belief," admonishing that it should be "said daily and acted on always."

> *"I understand L.L.L. to be the symbol or sign for three things which I must never neglect, and these things are – Lead, Log and Look-Out.*
> *"I believe in the Lead, as it warns me against dangers which the eye cannot see.*
> *"I believe in the Log, as it checks my distance run.*
> *"I believe in the Look-Out, as it warns me against dangers to be seen.*
> *"The Lead warns me against dangers invisible, the Log warns me against false distances, and the Look-Out warns me against dangers visible. And I earnestly resolve, and openly declare, that as I hope to sail my ship in safety on the ocean, as I wish to spare the lives of my fellow creatures at sea, and as I wish to go in safety all my days, so will I steadfastly practice that which I believe."* ≋

1870

RULES FOR WOODEN VESSELS

In June 1869 the Board of Marine Underwriters recognized *The Record* as the only approved American publication of the survey and classification of ships. And, as a result of a collaborative effort between the inspectors of various marine insurance company underwriters and the American Shipmasters' Association, *Rules for the Survey and Classing of Wooden Vessels* were formally published in 1870, appearing as part of *The Record*.

However, ship operators had begun to realize the virtues of iron-hulled ships, particularly their durability and strength. Moreover, shipbuilders discovered that iron plates, fastened together by riveting, eliminated a difficulty that had plagued construction

THEO. B. BLEECKER, JR.
President: 1871-1879; 1886-1898

of large wooden ships since the days of the early Phoenicians. Planks running end-to-end, from bow to stern, had an inherent weakness to the tensile and compressive stresses encountered at sea. ≋

6

1877

RULES FOR IRON VESSELS

Economics also played a critical role in the move from wood to iron. Iron ships were cheaper to build and returned a higher margin of profit than wooden vessels. In 1877, the American Shipmasters' Association published its first *Rules for the Survey and Classing of Iron Vessels.*

The 179-foot YANTIC built at the Navy Yard Philadelphia and powered by engines from Merrick and Sons.

Twelve years later a revised copy of the Rules was forwarded to the Hon. Benjamin F. Tracy, Secretary for the US Navy, for the consideration and approval of the US Navy Department. His response included the following extract:

"In this connection it is deemed proper to say that the Department is of the opinion that vessels built in accordance with the Rules above referred to, modified as suggested in the report of said board, would be useful as aux-iliary naval cruisers in time of war or in cases of emergency."

This response presaged the future role that would be played by the organization during the First and Second World Wars. And more than a century later, ABS and the US Navy would be working closely to develop specific technical criteria and Rules for naval vessels. ≋

1890

The next logical step in the evolution of shipbuilding was the use of steel, an alloy of iron that is lighter in weight, yet stronger than the base metal. With this development came the *Rules for Building and Classing Steel Vessels*. First published in 1890, these *Rules* have been updated and expanded on an annual basis and continue to provide marine engineers, naval architects, shipbuilders and shipowners with world-recognized standards for the design and construction of all types of marine vessels.

COLUMBIA – the first vessel with electric lights. Three generators were installed under the direction of Thomas A. Edison.

Steel had not been overlooked in the earlier *Rules*. They had stressed that the American Shipmasters' Association would "allow vessels built for classification...of steel a general weight reduction of twenty percent from the scantlings required for vessels built of iron." The statement was followed, however, by a list of exceptions.

In 1891, the American Shipmasters' Association published its initial set of *Rules for the Installation of Electric Lighting and Power Apparatus on Shipboard*. These Rules were the outgrowth of more than 10 years of experience with shipboard electric lighting, beginning with the steamship *COLUMBIA* in 1880. In that year *COLUMBIA*, which had been built to American Shipmasters' Association Class, became not only the first commercial vessel with incandescent electric lighting, but the first commercial installation of electric lighting.

A report of that time states: "The first electric plant that was ever put into operation in the hands of strangers was on the steamship *COLUMBIA* and was installed under directions from Mr. Edison."

Constructed in Mr. Edison's Menlo Park, New Jersey, laboratory, each of the three generators installed on the vessel was capable of supplying electricity to 60 lamps of 16 candlepower each. After completing her delivery voyage around Cape Horn to the US West Coast, the vessel's chief engineer reported "I have now 115 lamps in circuit, and have up-to-date run 415 hours and 45 minutes without one lamp giving out." The plant remained in service for more than 15 years with no need for significant repairs.

Several other installations were made shortly afterward as the use of incandescent lights on merchant ships spread rapidly. ≋

Steamship COLUMBIA delivered in 1880.

1891

OCEAN MAIL ACT

On 3 March 1891, the United States Congress enacted the Ocean Mail Act, requiring that mail service vessels "be of the highest rating known to maritime commerce." The US Solicitor General authorized the American Shipmasters' Association to survey and rate the first vessels built for transatlantic service under the Act, after learning from iron and steel vessel owners and other maritime industry leaders that existing Association Rules were already consistent with the new measure.

The ST. LOUIS, launched in 1894, had a length of 554 feet and propulsion machinery supplying 20,000 horsepower.

RULES FOR STEAM VESSELS

Also, with the advancement of steam propulsion, the Association assisted industry by addressing the technical aspects of this propulsive alternative with the publication in 1891 of *Rules for the Construction, Survey and Classification of Machinery and Boilers for Steam Vessels.*

Whether driven by propellers or sidewheels, early steam powered vessels had experienced a number of casualties as poorly constructed boilers caused frequent explosions and fires resulting in the loss of many lives. Figures dating back to 1832 showed that 14 percent of the steamships placed in operation were destroyed by boiler explosions, the direct result of a complexity of factors including poor workmanship and a lack of inspection laws.

In 1838, Congress enacted the Steamboat Inspection Service with the power to license masters, mates and engineers, as well as to appoint inspectors of boilers and vessels. This government initiative proved to be of little help. The incidence of boiler explosions aboard ship continued to increase.

An 1852 reorganization of this government service also proved ineffective. So it was that, at the time of its founding in 1861, the American Shipmasters' Association became the only effective organization in the United States that promoted safety of life at sea and upheld a standard of efficiency among the seagoing officer personnel. ≋

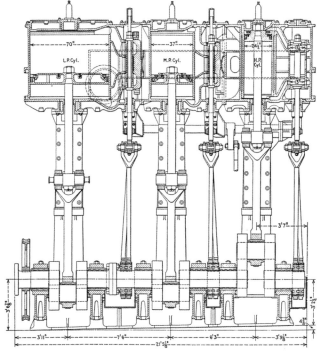

—Longitudinal Section Through Triple-Expansion Reciprocating Steam Engine

1892

FIRST TECHNICAL ADVISORY COMMITTEE ESTABLISHED

ANTON RAVEN
President: 1899-1916

Seeking further technical assistance with its responsibilities, the Shipmasters' Association, in December 1892, formed its first committee, known as the Advisory Council of Engineering and Marine Architects. The group was composed of prominent naval architects and marine engineers from industry and the US Navy, as well as academics from the University of Glasgow, Scotland, and Stevens Institute of Technology in Hoboken, New Jersey.

This council set the pattern for the formation of many subsequent technical committees devoted to particular subject areas: naval architecture, marine engineering, electrical engineering, and materials among them. Most important, however, was the fact that these committees consisted of members drawn from industry, giving them a voice in the determination of the Rules applied to their field. The result was a strong means of self-regulation in the areas of ship design and construction.

One of history's most unusual bulk carriers, the whalebacks were built in the 1880s and 1890s to carry grain and iron ore on the Great Lakes.

The 1892 Council served as a consulting group on the choice of material, the design, and the construction of iron and steel vessels, and their machinery, as well as making suggestions for the further improvement to the *Rules*. ≋

1898

NAME CHANGED TO AMERICAN BUREAU OF SHIPPING

Some years earlier, in 1884, the Association purchased the goodwill and title to *The American Lloyd's Universal Register*, a listing of ships, to consolidate it with the *Record*.

This was an indication that the Shipmasters' Association was changing. There was less emphasis on the qualifications of shipboard personnel and more on the ship itself.

This fundamental change in the day-to-day operation of the organization set the stage for its transition into a society solely dedicated to the classification of ships.

To more accurately describe the shift in its activity, a name change for the organization was needed. The American Shipmasters' Association adopted the name American Bureau of Shipping, or "ABS," as it was quickly labeled, on 26 September 1898, by authority from the Supreme Court of the State of New York.

Shortly thereafter, in May 1900, the issuance of the 6,807th Commission of Competency, to Captain Stanley Amsbury, brought the ABS involvement in examining ship's officers to an end. ≋

14

1916

REORGANIZATION OF ABS

The early 1900s were a time of change for ABS and its relation with the shipping industry. As the new organization grew, American Bureau of Shipping executives faced tough decisions that would shape its future course and identity. In July 1915, the management established a Reorganization Committee to decide how the Bureau could best be structured to serve the US maritime industry.

One major question faced by the Committee and the Bureau was how to respond to an approach from the London-based Lloyd's Register of Shipping proposing a merger between the two societies. Lloyd's Register was already established worldwide and had classed a number of American ships.

Opinions both pro and con were aired at a special October 1915 meeting, attended by 20 key individuals representing shipping companies, shipbuilders, engineering firms, steel companies, marine underwriters, and others with a vital interest in the future of the American maritime industry.

Some felt that Lloyd's should be the classification society, or that the United States society should merge with it, because they believed London was the place for insurance in the shipping industry. Other opinions, however, were just as strongly in favor of an American classification society.

The latter group predominated. The Committee found there was "a strong and insistent demand for an American Classification Association" on the part of American shipowners, builders, and underwriters.

A shipping company representative said, "We want a national standard organization in this country, and we would go in for it just as hard as we can." An underwriter added, "I would regret, and I think it would be a sad day for this country, if we had to depend absolutely on London for insurance. I hope to

STEVENSON TAYLOR
President: 1916-1926

16

US-built and flagged ships of the period, such as the 5,411 ton, 1919-built PAN ATLANTIC, would continue to be classed by a national standards organization, ABS.

see the day when all such insurance will be written in New York." A shipbuilder added, "We have the nucleus of a good institution in this Bureau."

Perhaps the point that weighed most heavily in the decision came with a hypothetical question posed by the committee to a representative of Lloyd's who was visiting the US at that time. "Suppose an American naval architect designs an improvement on existing designs for a ship; can the American Committee pass upon such a new design for classification?" The answer was, "The plans must be sent to London for approval."

To bolster its organization, the American Bureau of Shipping, in May 1916, bought the *Great Lakes Register*, which had been formed in Illinois in 1896 for the registry and classification of vessels in Great Lakes Service. The organization continued operation as the ABS Great Lakes Department. ≈

The direction was clear and, at a meeting of the Board of Managers in February 1916, a path of autonomy was chosen. A wide-ranging reorganization was decided, and a new ABS president elected, Stevenson Taylor, a prominent shipbuilder. The revised Constitution and Bylaws that were introduced provided a firm administrative footing for the Bureau until almost the end of the century.

1917

The American Bureau of Shipping reorganization plan also gained strength through an agreement made in January 1917 with the British Corporation for the Survey and Registry of Shipping, a classification society founded 27 years earlier in Scotland. This arrangement with the British Corporation allowed ABS to adopt its *Rules for the Construction of Steel Ships*, believed to be the best standards and practices of the time.

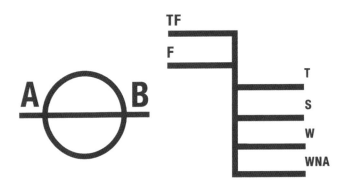

The Plimsoll Line to mark the draft limit first appeared on ships in the 1870s. It was adopted by 30 nations in 1930.

The agreement also included the reciprocal use of each organization's surveyors, and was probably ABS' first effort to promote classification on an international level. It also permitted an interchange of ideas that were advantageous to owners and builders in both countries.

Because the United States at that time had not enacted a Load Line Law, the arrangement with the British Corporation started the process toward international recognition of load lines for ABS-classed ships.

The load line, which signifies a vessel's draft limit, first began appearing on British merchant ships in the 1870s after a Member of Parliament, Samuel Plimsoll, worked long and hard to have the hull marking required by law. Known as the Plimsoll Line as a result, this mark spread to other maritime nations in the period until 1930, when delegates from 30 countries adopted an International Load Line Convention.

ABS played a vital role in the discussions when, as a member of the United States delegation, it explained technical aspects of load lines that remain the basis of those in effect today. According to terms of a 1966 Convention, the special markings on the hull are needed to register a ship in most ports around the world. The governments of almost 100 nations have subsequently authorized ABS to assign load lines on their behalf to vessels in their registry.

An agreement similar to that reached with the British Corporation concerning the use of surveyors was made with Registro Italiano Navale of Italy in 1918. The following year a similar agreement was forged with Teikoku Kaiji Kyokai, the Imperial Japanese Marine Corporation, now known as Nippon Kaiji Kyokai, or Class NK.

DEVELOPMENTS IN PROPULSION

1917 was also notable as the year in which the Bureau first included requirements for internal combustion engines within its Rules. Diesel engines were in their infancy but the selection of diesel installations began to increase rapidly from this time, both in direct drive and electric drive configurations.

Changes were also taking place in the design of steam driven machinery. Most ships were powered by Scotch boiler-driven steam reciprocating engines. However, the demand for new vessels to meet the wartime emergency fleet program outstripped the nation's ability to manufacture sufficient Scotch boilers and reciprocating engines. Production capability shifted to the construction of double-reduction geared turbines and watertube boilers. This shift was dramatic. By 1918, more than half of all boilers provided under the wartime emergency fleet program were of the new watertube variety.

Ironically, the massive shipbuilding program undertaken during the Second World War saw a return to steam reciprocating engines although the watertube boiler was retained. The reason was one of simple expediency since all steam turbine production capacity was allocated to the US Navy for the higher speed combatant vessels.

Several companies were able to build reciprocating machinery to an early British design but there was no longer any US capacity for building Scotch boilers leading to the fitting of more than 2,700 watertube boiler fired steam reciprocating engines on the famed Liberty ship fleet. ≋

1918

WORLD WAR I: A PERIOD OF INTENSE ACTIVITY

Both as a result of the reorganization and a resurgence of shipbuilding in the United States during World War I, ABS experienced a period of intense activity and growth in the immediate post-war period. The newly reorganized ABS had classed the majority of American ships built to meet the demands of the war, cementing its position as an irreplaceable component of the American maritime industry. This position was reinforced over the next ten years as the number of American ship-owners using ABS services continued to increase. ≋

The S.S. ABRAHAM LINCOLN on a trial run in September 1919.

1920

MERCHANT MARINE ACT

The American Bureau of Shipping was officially recognized by the United States government in the Merchant Marine Act of 1920. The legislation required that, in work involving a classification organization, every governmental agency in the United States would turn to ABS.

The 210-foot, 1,000-gt STANDARD SERVICE, built in 1923 for Standard Oil Company of California, now Chevron, was the world's first diesel-electric tanker.

Built to ABS class for Great Lakes Service in July 1925, the 573-foot T.W. ROBINSON had the first turbo-electric drive.

In 1921, having established itself as the American classification society, the American Bureau of Shipping began regular publication of the *Bulletin* to supply up-to-date information on the scope of services provided.

Statistics published in the March/April 1922 *Bulletin* showed the significant turnaround in ABS' progress since the reorganization in 1916. At that time ABS had in class only eight and one-half percent of all American-classed tonnage. By year-end 1921, the society classed approximately 80 percent.

Recognizing its growing importance within the marine industry, the Bureau instituted a system of cash prizes for scholarships at the six leading universities within the US at which Naval Architecture and Marine Engineering were taught. The initiative began a tradition that has continued, fostering excellence in these disciplines that are so important to continuing innovation within the marine industry. Although the initial awards were restricted to US educational establishments and American citizens, the scholarship program has been steadily extended to universities and students throughout the world. ≋

CHARLES A. MCALLISTER
President: 1926-1932

1928

AMERICAN BUREAU OF AIRCRAFT FOUNDED

ABS management looked toward the developing aviation industry, and in 1926 considered expanding its activities to include the classification and registration of planes and airships. As a result, ABS, along with all other major classification societies, participated in the International Aviation Alliance Conference held in France in June 1927.

The following year, ABS founded the American Bureau of Aircraft to cooperate with municipal, state, and federal agencies for the benefit of the aviation industry. However the venture proved short-lived as subsequent developments brought the regulation of this industry under federal control, thus supplanting the need for a private regulatory organization. ≋

In October 1927, ABS headquarters were moved to 24-26 Old Slip in New York City.

MALOLO, built to ABS class in 1927 for the Matson Navigation Company, had first-class sleeping accommodations for 650 passengers. Steam turbines producing a total of 25,000 shaft horsepower to twin screws, gave the 582-foot ship a cruising speed of 21 knots. MALOLO was designed by William Francis Gibbs, who later designed the famed UNITED STATES.

1931

WELDED BOILERS ACCEPTED

During the early 1930s, ABS approved the general use of electric welding for the fabrication of various major machinery components. The US Navy and industry had conducted considerable research into the use of welding for the fabrication of watertube boiler drums, examining the completed welds with X-rays. ABS and the Navy accepted the use of welded boiler construction as the industry standard in 1931. The technique and required survey procedures became part of ABS Rules. All boilers constructed for the Maritime Commission's World War II ship-building program were in accordance with these Rules. ≋

The twin-screw diesel-powered CITY OF NEW YORK passenger liner leaving port.

1936

MERCHANT MARINE ACT BOOSTS SHIPBUILDING

The landmark US Merchant Marine Act of 1936 provided an immediate stimulus to the building of merchant ships. The merchant fleet at the time consisted of many ships built during World War I. A program calling for the replacement of the existing aging vessels with newer, more efficient ships – at the rate of 50 per year – was undertaken by the Maritime Commission created by the 1936 legislation. Over the course of a decade, this program brought about a variety of changes in the design and construction of ships' hulls, machinery, boilers and equipment, all classed by ABS. Rules were modified to take into account increasing boiler pressures and steam temperatures. ≈

One of 14 vessels of the Exporter design owned by the American Export Lines, the S.S. EXEMPLAR was 473 feet long and 9,900 deadweight tons (dwt).

1937

FIRST AUTOMATIC WELDING PROCESS APPROVED

The 1936 ABS Rules were the first among major classification societies to stipulate that welding would be accepted for all parts of the hull. Detailed requirements for the approval of electrodes were included. Then, in 1937, the first automatic welding process was approved and ABS began classing tankers, some larger than 18,000 deadweight tons capacity, with tank spaces of all-welded construction.

The CHARLES S. JONES remains decorated following launching ceremonies at Sparrows Point, Maryland in October 1941.

Accompanying the use of advanced welding in ship construction was ABS' establishment of its own metallurgical laboratory. The main function of the lab was the investigation of weld samples submitted by various shipyards seeking ABS approval for welding processes, joint designs and other procedures involving materials. ≋

ABS started its own metallurgical laboratory to test weld samples and became more involved in materials testing and investigation.

1941

Just before the start of World War II, the Maritime Commission's long-range program to help restore the United States merchant fleet had included the well-known C-1, C-2, and C-3 cargo ships. ABS was involved in the approval of these new designs. During the War years, a total of 868 such vessels, amounting to almost 5,000,000 gross tons, were built to ABS class.

To meet this unprecedented growth in shipbuilding activity, ABS expanded its workforce – in particular, its staff of surveyors. A particular focus was the emergency program for the construction of the famous Liberty Ship, or EC-2 (E for emergency, C for cargo), as it was officially titled.

This renowned 417-foot long, 10,500 deadweight ton vessel was not the sleekest looking cargo ship afloat, and attracted uncomplimentary descriptions. For example, President Franklin D. Roosevelt nicknamed it the "Ugly Duckling." But,

47 Beaver Street became headquarters for ABS in April 1941, when more room was needed.

A C-1 type, SANTA CRUZ, had a length of 395 feet with a displacement of 12,875 tons. Propulsion came from 4,400 shaft horsepower steam turbines.

whatever its name, the ship was powered by a triple-expansion, steam (220 psi) reciprocating engine that developed 2,500 horsepower and provided a top speed of approximately 10 to 11 knots in calm seas. Most important, the ships produced a necessary lifeline for the tons of war supplies needed by the Allied nations.

Established shipyards in the US were being used to construct naval vessels, so some 18 new shipyards, with over 200 slipways, were developed to build the Liberties. In many cases the vessels were under construction as the shipyard itself was being completed.

The C-2, JOHN LAND, was 459 feet long, with a displacement of 13,893 tons, and a steam turbine propulsion unit of 6,600 shaft horsepower.

The C-3, S.S. PIKE had a length of 465 feet and a displacement of 17,675 tons. A steam turbine delivered 9,350 shaft horsepower.

As more ships were built, production time per vessel was reduced. Large sub-assemblies, welded elsewhere in the yard, were brought to the slipway for final assembly, in some cases setting unprecedented production speeds. One complete Liberty ship was built in four days, 15 hours and 30 minutes. Such a schedule, whether four and one-half days per vessel or 17 days as one shipyard was averaging, kept the ABS surveyors active in their efforts to assure quality of workmanship at every point. ≋

One of 2,710 Liberty ships built in the United States during World War II.

1942

The demand on the shipyards and ABS surveyors was unrelenting. In 1939, ABS had 92 exclusive surveyors on its staff. At the peak of the wartime shipbuilding program in 1944, the survey staff had increased to 479.

Before the end of the War, some 2,710 of the Liberty ships, totaling 19,467,486 gross tons, were built to ABS class. Of these, two were named for American Bureau of Shipping past presidents: *S.S. STEVENSON TAYLOR*, and the *S.S. CHARLES S. MCALLISTER*. Another was named *S.S. FRANK H. EVERS*, after a principal surveyor for ABS.

The larger and faster Victory cargo ship followed the Liberties on the slipways in 1944, with 531 totaling more than 4 million gross tons built during the War to ABS classification. The Bureau participated extensively in developing the new design, with ABS

Following the Liberty ship were the larger and faster Victory ships with 6,000 and 8,500 shaft horsepower propulsion units.

President J. Lewis Luckenbach taking a close personal interest. Of these 10,712 deadweight ton, 436 feet long vessels, 272 had steam turbine engines of 6,000 shaft horsepower and 258 had turbines developing 8,500 shaft horsepower. One of the vessels had a diesel propulsion system installed.

In all, some 5,171 seagoing vessels of many types, including troop transports, ore carriers, small and large cargo ships and oil tankers, but excluding naval vessels, were produced in this shipbuilding program up to the end of 1945. These aggregated more than 38 million gross tons and all were built to Bureau classification. In addition, there were many special types of vessels built for the Maritime Commission to Bureau standards. ≋

1943

During the War period, 525 T-2 tankers with turbo-electric propulsion, totaling 5,422,819 gross tons, were constructed to ABS class. Perhaps the best known of these 500 foot workhorses was *SCHENECTADY.*

In January 1943, after it had been put through sea trials, the ship was tied up at the outfitting dock along the Willamette River in Portland, Oregon. Suddenly, with the sound of an explosion heard for several miles, the deck and both sides of the vessel fractured just aft of the bridge superstructure. The instantaneous fracture was total, extending to the turn of the bilge on both sides. Only the bottom plating held.

The ship jack-knifed. The center portion of the vessel rose out of the river to such a position – with the bow and the stern resting on the bottom – that no water entered the hull.

Welding was still considered a relatively new procedure for ships. Although the Bureau had first included guidelines for electric and gas welding of relatively minor structural components within a vessel's hull in its 1927 Rules, it was not until the late 1930s that all-welded merchant ships entered service. Most of the Liberty ships were welded.

Early in the War some merchant vessels experienced inexplicable fractures that were believed to be related to welding. As a result, in April 1943, the Secretary of the US Navy established a Board of Investigation to inquire into the design and methods of construction of welded steel merchant vessels. This Board included top-level representatives from the Navy, Coast Guard, the Maritime Commission and the American Bureau of Shipping.

The investigation was extensive. More than $100 million was spent. Examinations were made on various types of vessels known to have had structural failures. Included were: four Great Lakes ore carriers, 20 Liberty ships, six T-2 tankers, three C-4 troop carriers, 21 Victory ships and one C-2 refrigerated cargo ship.

The INGLEWOOD HILLS, a T-2 tanker, was one of more than 500 built to carry fuels to Allied Nations.

The ships were subjected to a variety of tests: full-scale hull bending studies in still water; determination of locked-in stresses, including those caused by temperature variations during assembly; and examination of thermal stresses while in service, among others.

These studies found that fractures in the welded ships were caused by steel that was "notch-sensitive" at operating temperatures, a susceptibility that could be caused by high sulfur and phosphorous content. A notch in this sense is a discontinuity in the metal, which results in high stress concentration.

The research report also cited design-related structural discontinuities, such as hatch openings, vents and other interruptions in the structure.

As a means of preventing the propagation of cracks that might originate in certain places, riveted "crack arrestors" were installed. In addition, the original square cargo hatch corners were rounded and installed on vessels under construction, as well as those already completed.

Sharp structural discontinuities and abrupt section design changes in the vessel were avoided wherever possible. These safety precautions helped reduce the number of hull fractures from 140 per month in March 1944 to less than 20 per month two years later.

This thorough investigation solved the brittle fracturing problem associated with the all-welded ship. Fortunately only eight of the thousands of ships built by the Maritime Commission were lost during the War as a direct result of brittle fracture. ≈

Attesting to the robustness of the war-built Liberty ships, the S.S. JEREMIAH O'BRIEN remained in operating condition almost 60 years after delivery.

J. Lewis Luckenbach

President: 1933-1950
Chairman: 1950-1951

(Received "Distinguished Public Service Award" from US Department of the Navy
for meritorious services during World War II as President of ABS.)

1945

For the American Bureau of Shipping, the post-War period signaled a move from its Beaver Street headquarters in New York to larger quarters in a nearby building at 45 Broad Street. This move coincided with the assignment of exclusive ABS surveyors to key overseas ports.

This global expansion had its origins during the War. It had become necessary to assign surveyors to the Armed Forces for work with the, then existing, War Shipping Administration. This group was responsible for surveying all vessels, particularly those damaged in action.

The duties included checking for seaworthiness and arranging for any emergency repairs necessary for the vessel's trip home. The surveyors assigned to this job followed the Allied invasion of Europe from North Africa and Italy. By the end of the War, these surveyors were located in Genoa and Naples, where they promptly established ABS offices.

Before the end of World War II, ABS bought this eight-story building at 45 Broad Street in New York City.

As peace returned, ABS representation expanded considerably overseas. The United States government sold hundreds of ABS-classed surplus vessels, mostly Liberties and T-2 tankers, to European allies who had lost most of their fleets. Because they were sold on long-term agreements, the Merchant Marine Act required that any ship on which the US government held a mortgage be kept in ABS class. As a result, the number of exclusive ABS offices quickly expanded from Western Europe, into Africa, Asia and South America, turning what had been a national classification society into a worldwide operation.

The 579-foot PRESIDENT CLEVELAND, American President Lines, incorporated extensive use of aluminum in the deck houses.

This expansion was further fueled by a worldwide demand for new ships, many of which were contracted to be built outside the United States by organizations that were long standing clients of the Bureau. This post-War trend towards ship construction in non-US shipyards, some of which had, ironically, adopted the production line methods pioneered in US shipyards that produced the Liberty ships, proved irreversible. The transformation of the American Bureau of Shipping into the global organization known as ABS had begun. ≈

Designed to support the Korean War effort, the 564 ft, 20 knot Mariner class established new technical standards and provided decades of commercial serivce.

1952

New technologies, the result of wartime research, were being adopted by the shipbuilding industry. A notable example was the application of aluminum to vessel structures. Shortly after the end of the War, ABS received proposals for the building of two ocean-going ore carriers to be of all-aluminum alloy construction, although the project never materialized.

A comprehensive testing program undertaken by the Bureau determined that riveted construction using aluminum alloys could not be caulked satisfactorily and that welded connections did not offer adequate strength, using the techniques available at that time. These drawbacks limited the application of the new material but, in 1946, ABS approved the use of aluminum for the riveted upper house and stack installation on the Delta Steamship's Del Sud-class of vessels built at Ingalls Shipbuilding Corporation.

Aluminum was used more extensively in the design of *PRESIDENT WILSON* and *PRESIDENT CLEVELAND* for American President Lines. But it was the 1952 construction of the United States Lines' *S.S. UNITED STATES* by the Newport News Shipbuilding and Dry Dock Company that brought extensive use of aluminum alloy material to the superstructure of the vessel.

During the building of this vessel, ABS spent much time reviewing the details of scantlings. Inspection focused on aluminum rivets, the materials used for insulation between joints of dissimilar metals, and the wide variety of special connections required.

S.S. UNITED STATES was the first of what became a venerable list of renowned large passenger liners with which ABS became identified during the post-War years. Another, the *S.S. FRANCE*, was the longest passenger liner in the world at the time. The vessel had an all-welded aluminum house structure, and was built to ABS class for the French

WALTER L. GREEN

President: 1950-1952
President and Chairman: 1952-1957
Chairman: 1957-1959

The US Lines' S.S. UNITED STATES and the American Export's S.S. INDEPENDENCE arriving together in New York harbor.

Line by the Chantiers de L'Atlantique shipyard in Saint Nazaire, France.

In Italy, some of the large luxury liners built to ABS requirements were *LEONARDO DA VINCI*, *CRISTOFORO COLOMBO*, *ANDREA DORIA*, *AUGUSTUS*, *GIULIO CESARE* and *MICHELANGELO*. Later the A/B Svenska Amerika-Linien liner *GRIPSHOLM* was also built to ABS class, as were *AMERICA* and her sister ships, *CONSTITUTION* and *INDEPENDENCE*, of the American Export Line and the luxurious *SANTA PAULA* and *SANTA ROSA* for Grace Line. ≈

With an overall length of 1,035 feet, the ABS-classed S.S. FRANCE, was announced as the world's longest liner when launched in 1960. This vessel also used aluminum extensively in the superstructure.

DAVID P. BROWN

President: 1957-1963
Chairman: 1963-1964

1953

INTERNATIONAL TECHNICAL COMMITTEES FORMED

With such rapid, worldwide expansion of ABS activities came the need to address the specific requirements of various countries. Building on its successful technical committee structure, ABS decided to establish similar international technical committees. Each of these groups has proved a valuable asset over the years by keeping ABS apprised of technical developments that might ultimately aid in Rule development.

The Italian and Belgian Technical Committees were the first to be established, consisting of persons prominent in the fields of naval architecture and marine engineering. In 1954, the Netherlands Technical Committee was formed, followed two years later by the French Technical Committee.

With ABS' increased representation in other countries, the advantages of these committees became readily apparent. Advances in the technology used in ship construction and related fields were being made across the globe. ABS responded by forming several new Special Committees and Panels to deal with these advancements.

Each unit had a specialty: reinforced plastic vessels for one, underwater systems for another. Still others focused on welding, single-point mooring, gears or propellers. Like the committees formed earlier, the groups included many of the most respected people in each specific field and gave them voices in the creation of the ABS Rules.

The ABS Rule Committee was structured so that, if a change in the Rules was proposed, it had to be submitted to the appropriate committee for review. If approved by that group, the suggested change was then submitted to the Committee on Naval Architecture if it concerned a vessel's hull, or the Committee on Engineering if it dealt with machinery.

When passed by either of these two committees, the proposal moved on to the Technical Committee. Approval by this body incorporated the change as part of the Rules. ≋

ARTHUR R. GATEWOOD

President: 1963-1964
Chairman: 1964

1961

FIRST NUCLEAR POWERED COMMERCIAL VESSEL BUILT TO ABS CLASS

To meet demands of the early 1960s, Rules were updated with the ABS *Guide for the Classification of Nuclear Ships*, used to class *N.S. SAVANNAH*, the first nuclear-powered commercial ship in the world. ABS chaired the Atomic Energy Panel convened by the Society of Naval Architects and Marine Engineers and helped draft a precedent-setting report: "Safety Considerations Affecting the Design and Installation of Water-Cooled and Water-Moderated Reactors on Merchant Ships."

A 9,830 deadweight ton vessel, *N.S. SAVANNAH* had a length of 545 feet and a beam of 78 feet. The single-screw ship was powered by a pressurized water reactor nuclear plant that generated steam for a two-cycle turbine unit developing 22,000 shaft horsepower. From 1962 to 1970, the ship traveled over 500,000 miles. With a 99.88 percent availability, the service record of the nuclear propulsion system was considered almost flawless. The *N.S. SAVANNAH*, with Savannah, Georgia as its port of registry, was owned by the United States Department of Commerce, and operated by First Atomic Ship Transport, Inc.

The N.S. SAVANNAH, the first nuclear-powered merchant ship in the world, gets a royal New York welcome while moving up the Hudson River.

Special 60-foot barges are quickly stowed on a LASH (lighter aboard ship) vessel.

tanker lengths and capacities. When the capacities began to exceed 300,000 deadweight tons, the term "ultra large crude carriers," or ULCCs, was applied.

In 1964, the first LASH (lighter aboard ship) vessel, a new shipping concept, was put into operation. The LASH vessel was designed as a courier between river systems in different parts of the world. Once unloaded from the ship, there was reduced time pressure to unload or load the barge itself as it would no longer delay the ship.

An 895-foot long LASH vessel could carry 89 60-foot barges, each lifted on board by a 2,000 ton capacity elevator on the stern of the vessel. The larger, 97-foot *SEABEE* barge, carried on a vessel of a slightly different design concept, opened new markets and distribution points where only a marginal port facility – or often none at all had previously existed.

Each barge was considered a separate vessel, subject to inspection, and ABS provided both classification and assignment of load-line services. ≋

One successful vessel was not enough to propel nuclear-powered commercial vessels into seagoing facts of life. Yet early in 1977 one enterprising shipowner signed a letter of intent (never converted) with a United States shipyard to build three nuclear-powered, "very large crude carriers," or VLCCs, as they were called in those days of ever-increasing

1968

THE ARIZONA PROJECT

Tankers kept growing in size. Chevron Shipping Company, in the late 1960s, ordered six tankers of approximately 200,000 deadweight tons built to ABS class. The maritime industry had little experience with such huge vessels. As a result, ABS joined Chevron and a research team at the University of Arizona to develop a computerized technique for analyzing the entire complex structure of one of these large tankers under expected service conditions.

The program, which included the University's aerospace and mechanical engineering departments, led to the creation of a program called DAISY (Displacement Automated Integrated System). A finite element displacement method of investigation capable of analyzing plated structures throughout an entire ship, *DAISY* was subsequently used in the design review and analyses of LNG vessels, containerships, mobile offshore drilling units, large tankers, bulk carriers,

As tanker size increased dramatically in the late 1960s and early 1970s, ABS was the first class society to develop and apply finite element analysis to their design.

ANDREW NEILSON

President: 1964-1965
President and Chairman: 1965-1970
Chairman: 1970-1971

general cargo ships and barges. The structures analyzed ranged in size from a hatch cover to a complete hull. Chevron's 212,000 dwt *JOHN A. McCONE*, built by Kockums Mekaniska of Sweden and delivered in 1969, was the first vessel in the world to be subjected to a complete ship finite element analysis. Although the American Bureau of Shipping had well-established technology research programs, the escalation in ship size which began in the 1960s led to a further expansion of this activity.

In the early 1960s, ABS opened a total of 18 new, exclusive offices in 13 nations, increased its personnel by almost 50 percent and more than doubled the size of its technical staff.

MODU RULES AND EXPANSION OFFSHORE

One consequence of this expanded technical capability was the development of the first *Rules for Building and Classing Offshore Mobile Drilling Units* in 1968. This followed a request of the industry's mobile offshore operators committee. Offshore drilling structures had been in existence for many years, but installations had remained in relatively shallow water. It was not until 1947 that the first well was drilled from a platform out of sight of land. An ABS-classed barge, moored alongside the pile-supported platform, served as crew quarters.

The first mobile offshore drilling rig, a pontoon-supported unit, began operating in 1949. The Rules published 19 years later covered both floating and bottom-supported units and included the latest data covering wave height, wind speed and stability needed to determine whether a drilling structure was eligible for classification. When the International Maritime Consultative Organization (IMCO), an adjunct of the United Nations, prepared its *Rules for Mobile Offshore Drilling Units*, the ABS 1968 Rules were used as a basis. (IMCO has since been shortened to IMO). ≋

Drilled in 1947 by Kerr-McGee Oil Industries, the first well out of sight of land produced more than one million barrels of oil from beneath the Gulf of Mexico during a 20-year operating life.

1969

THE MANHATTAN PROJECT

In 1969, ABS contributed to the pioneering Arctic venture that came to be known as the Manhattan Project. In an effort to determine the feasibility of shipping oil from the new, large Alaskan fields, eastbound to Atlantic destinations, the ABS-classed tanker *MANHATTAN* underwent radical structural modification, creating the largest ice breaking cargo ship to ever enter service. With the capability to navigate in heavy ice, the vessel made a single, successful trip through the Northwest Passage, an east-to-west voyage from Baffin Bay, through Lancaster Sound and Viscount Melville Sound, to the Beaufort Sea and the oil fields at Prudhoe Bay. The entire trip was made at about 75 degrees north latitude, in icy waters well above the Arctic Circle.

Although demonstrating the technological feasibility of such an operation, commercial considerations were never similarly satisfied and the idea was abandoned. However, important data was gathered by ABS that was subsequently applied to the design and construction of smaller ships earmarked for operation in extremely cold conditions.

The tanker MANHATTAN, with special ABS-approved structural changes, demonstrates its ice-breaking capabilities while crossing the Northwest Passage.

AND THE WORLD'S FASTEST CONTAINERSHIPS

The concept of carrying cargo in containers was developed in the United States to reduce ship time at dockside, cut the cost of cargo handling and prevent petty pilferage. The first vessel to carry containers, the IDEAL X on passage from Newark, New Jersey to Houston, Texas in April 1956, was classed by ABS. Many of the early containerships were converted World War II built vessels. A typical conversion involved both lengthening and widening the vessel to maximize stowage of the containers.

In the 1960s owners increasingly turned to purpose-designed ships culminating in a unique series of eight containerships built to ABS classification for Sea-Land Service, Inc. in 1969. Capable of carrying 1,138 containers, the 877 foot-long vessels were the Greyhounds of the North Atlantic. Twin-screw steam turbines generated 120,000 shaft horsepower to drive them as fast as 33 knots, the fastest in the world at the time, and a speed which had not been matched by any similar vessel by the turn of the century.

As an adjunct to the *Rules* covering the construction of the containerships themselves, ABS also formulated *Rules for the Certification of the Containers for Strength and Weather Tightness.* ≋

Sea-Land Service, Inc. operated eight high-speed, 27,358-dwt containerships of the design of the SEA-LAND RESOURCE. A twin-screw turbine drive provided an operating speed of 33 knots.

ROBERT T. YOUNG

President: 1970-1971
President and Chairman: 1971-1977
Chairman: 1977-1979

1970

The year 1970 was significant for ABS. The society classed 895 vessels of over 7 million gross tons, an increase of 40 percent over the previous year. Not only was the orderbook on the increase, so too were the size of vessels, particularly tankers, being ordered. In 1969 ABS had received a request to class a nearly 367,000 deadweight ton tanker – the largest ordered up to that time. Within months the vessel was upstaged by a contract for two 469,000 deadweight ton tankers to ABS class. During those heady days, ABS also participated in feasibility studies for the hull structure of tankers in the 750,000 and 1,000,000 deadweight ton categories.

In 1971, the 366,812-dwt NISSEKI MARU was the largest tanker in the world. It was nearly 1,138 feet long with a beam of 180 feet.

Such immense vessels were side-effects of political difficulties in the Middle East. The Suez Canal was closed, denying tankers easy access from the Mediterranean, Europe and North America to the Arabian Gulf-based oil ports. Much larger tankers made the prospect of carrying huge quantities of crude oil around the southern tip of Africa to the rest of the world appear economical.

The longer trip also placed an immediate constraint on the supply of tanker tonnage causing a sharp rise in charter rates. At its peak, the tanker boom offered enterprising owners the opportunity of paying off the entire cost of a new VLCC within the first year of operation.

An early example of ABS' diversified activity was its involvement in the construction of San Francisco's Golden Gate Bridge.

However, these behemoths would be severely restricted in their choice of discharge ports as, in most cases, the ships could no longer transit the same channels or harbors as their predecessors. Operating drafts had increased by up to 20 feet, requiring new deepwater berths. And a frenzy of ordering soon pushed the supply/demand imbalance in the reverse direction. The oversupply of tonnage and resultant plunge in tanker rates later in the decade would have profound implications on the shipping and shipbuilding industries, and on the fortunes of ABS, throughout the 1980s.

NEW SUBSIDIARY FORMED FOR NON-MARINE CONTRACTS

1971 saw the formation of ABS Worldwide Technical Services, Inc., a wholly owned subsidiary of the American Bureau of Shipping. Except for a small number of unusual cases, ABS had restricted its activities to marine classification. One such exception occurred in the early 1930s, when ABS inspected and witnessed testing of the steel and caissons used in the construction of the San Francisco Golden Gate and Oakland Bay bridges.

ABSTECH, an acronym for ABS Worldwide Technical Services, Inc., was established to offer independent inspection, certification and quality assurance services for industrial equipment. By 1976, its sixth full year of operation, ABSTECH had provided inspection and consulting services on 6,000 projects at heavy construction and petroleum industry work sites around the world.

ABSTECH also formed a subsidiary known as EXAM Company which used nondestructive testing techniques in its quality assurance pipeline inspection services. In a challenging project EXAM used radiographic techniques to inspect a 400-mile section of the Trans-Alaska pipeline. ≋

1971

LNG VESSEL ACTIVITY INCREASES

The shipbuilding boom of the early 1970s spilled over into the gas sector with intense demand for liquefied natural gas (LNG) carriers. The first vessel designed to carry liquefied gas, the C-1 cargo ship *NATALIE O. WARREN* was converted to Bureau standards in 1947. In the late 1950s to early 1960s the Bureau classed several vessels designed specifically for the carriage of liquefied petroleum gas (LPG).

The first vessel designed to carry liquefied petroleum gases was S.S. NATALIE O. WARREN, formerly the CAPE DIAMOND, a C-1 type cargo vessel built in 1944. The ship was converted to an LPG carrier in 1947.

By the 1970s gas carrier size requirements were steadily increasing, posing new challenges for the Bureau. Members of the ABS technical staff investigated the structural soundness of three 125,000 cubic meter LNG vessels built to ABS class, using three-dimensional finite element analysis under dynamic conditions. A proposed 160,000 cubic meter design was the subject of a similar analysis.

ABS has had wide experience with gas-carrying vessels. The 936-foot LNG LEO, with a capacity of 125,000 cubic meters, was one of two series of eight such vessels.

LNG is a liquefied form of methane gas that must be cooled to minus 162 degrees Celsius at atmospheric pressure to maintain that state. During the voyage some of the cargo is lost through evaporation, and the resulting gas can be used in the propulsion machinery. Some three decades of experience has proved the success of this technology.

Designing an effective containment system for the liquefied gas posed a significant challenge to the industry. Two basic types became the accepted alternatives – membrane tanks and self-supporting, independent tanks. Membrane tanks contain the LNG by using a thin, metallic shell or membrane. This is backed by a boxed construction containing the insulating material, and a secondary barrier. The construction must be able to transmit the static and dynamic loads to the ship's structure. The independent, self-supporting tank configuration is designed to withstand these loads in addition to providing the required insulation.

As new technology provided new variations on these methods for containing the liquefied gas, ABS remained in the forefront of technical research. It became the first society, and for many years was the only society, with practical experience in each of the alternative systems and their derivatives. ≋

1972

CLASSIFICATION GROWS

As the tanker-inspired shipbuilding boom continued, the number of ships classed by ABS continued to grow on an annual basis, far exceeding the amount dreamed of in the early years. By the end of 1972, the first of the elusive 100 million ton barriers was breached with a total 9,368 vessels aggregating 102 million deadweight tons in ABS class.

ABS has been certifying containers for more than 30 years.

With an increase in the number of container-carrying vessels, the ABS Container Certification program was also subject to rapid growth. 1972 saw an increase of 42 percent over the previous year, with ABS certifying 32 different design types in accordance with US Customs Requirements for Containers and the International Transport of Goods under cover of the Transporte Internationale de Routiers (TIR) Convention of 1959. This convention was designed to streamline international transport of freight via road and rail vehicles by simplifying customs requirements. ≋

1973

TUG-BARGE COMBINATION PROVIDES COST-SAVING

In later years this period of shipbuilding activity would be viewed as one of unparalleled technical innovation. The growth in the size of vessels – tankers, bulk carriers and containerships alike – took designers and classification societies into new territory for which there were no empirical guidelines. Innovation led to the development of composite vessels such as ore-bulk-oil (OBO) carriers; specialist roro car carriers; open hatch bulk carriers, designed for the efficient carriage of forest products; and a host of other specialist carriers. It marked the demise of the traditional general cargo ship that had been the mainstay of every shipping fleet.

PRESQUE ISLE, *a tug-barge combination designed for Great Lakes Service, is over 1,000 feet long.*

Without exception these technical developments were inspired by shipowners seeking operational and cost advantages. One of the more radical of these developments originated in the United States, driven by a desire to reduce crew costs. The Integrated Tug Barge (ITB) combination appealed to some shipowners as it offered the same carrying capacity as a conventional vessel with the manning requirements of a tug. The concept consisted of a fit-and-lock connection between the stern of the barge and the bow of the tug, forming a rigid unit capable of ocean going service.

A variation on this design was developed for service on the Great Lakes. This *PRESQUE ISLE* tug-and-barge combination, built to carry a refined pelletized iron ore known as taconite, had a barge length of 974 feet and a width of 104 feet. The notch in its stern was designed to fit the 140-foot *PRESQUE ISLE* tug. The unique vessel, capable of self-discharging at a rate of 10,000 tons per hour, measured over 1,000 feet from stem-to-stern and was constructed to ABS class. Other integrated tug-barge designs that underwent review at that time included a 12,000 cubic meter LNG carrier.

Meanwhile tanker orders continued to set new records. Twenty years earlier the 47,450 deadweight ton, ABS-classed

With a 1,244-foot length, a 93-foot draft and a deadweight of 472,292 tons, GLOBTIK LONDON and its sister ship GLOBTIK TOKYO, were the largest ships on the water in 1973. Also noteworthy was each vessel's speed of 15.5 knots.

SPYROS NIARCHOS, was proclaimed the world's largest tanker. Ten other ABS-classed ships had laid consecutive claim to that title, culminating with the delivery of the 476,292 deadweight ton *GLOBTIK LONDON*.

Going to the opposite extreme, ABS in 1973 published *Rules for Building and Classing Steel Vessels Under 61 Meters or 200 Feet in Length*. By then, the ABS *Rules for Building and Classing Steel Vessels* were also published in Greek, German and Portuguese. ≋

1974

A BUSY YEAR

Figures underscore the unprecedented growth of ABS, as well as the tremendous output of the shipbuilding industry in the early to mid-1970s. For example, at the end of 1970, the aggregate gross tonnage of ships under ABS classification totaled approximately 49 million tons. By the end of 1974, this had burgeoned to more than 82 million gt with a further 3,185 vessels aggregating over 33 million gt on the orderbook.

Much of this growth was attributable to the boom in tanker construction. But the demand for the new, more efficient, specialized ships was insatiable. An indication of the on-going expansion of the containership segment could be found in the international orderbook as 1974 drew to a close. Shipyards were building approximately 200 container-carrying vessels and ABS certified 32,000 containers during the year, a year-on-year increase of 16 percent.

HUGHES GLOMAR EXPLORER drillship built at Sun Shipping and Drydock in Chester, Pennsylvania.

Increased activity in the search for oil and gas offshore saw a similar increase in ABS-classed offshore units. By the end of 1974, ABS had classed 145 mobile offshore drilling units of various types, and had a further 93 units either on order or under construction.

The drilling units in class at this time came in a variety of designs. Column-stabilized drilling units employed a design that relied on ballast tanks within the three to eight cylindrically shaped columns to support the platform, and a grid of cylinders that formed a lower hull to provide stability. Self-elevating units raised or lowered the hull above the waterline on legs that, although solidly planted on the bottom, could be easily lifted when the job was completed. Such rigs are known to the industry as "jackups" because their operating principle is similar to that of an automobile jack.

Yet another of the mobile offshore units ABS had classed by 1974 was the drillship. These vessels drill through a hole in the bottom of the hull and are able to work in ocean depths of many thousands of feet. Such a unit is kept on-site, despite the effects of wind and waves, by a computer-controlled system known as "dynamic positioning."

EMBRACING COMPUTERS

At this time computers were becoming more and more important to the management and operations of ABS. The period saw the development of a suite of programs able to analyze such elements as longitudinal strength, vessel stability, vibration, cargo gear, sea loads and ship motion, among others.

By March 1976, ABS demonstrated its leadership in the application of this fledgling technology with the formation of a new subsidiary, ABS Computers, Inc. better known by the acronym, ABSCOMP. The new unit offered data processing, analysis and other computer services and business systems support to ABS and its subsidiaries.

Harnessing the power of computers was to become a preoccupation for ABS over the coming years as it sought to use computing power to improve its own operating efficiencies and also to lead the development of new standards for the marine and offshore industries.

These pioneering steps taken in the early 1970s provided the genesis for the revolutionary ABS SafeHull dynamic based design evaluation system, and ABS SafeNet, a complete life cycle fleet information management system, released to industry in the 1990s.

In the early days, ABS initially handled the complex calculations for research and development, plan review and other

ABSCOMP operator reviews hard copy produced from data appearing on console screens in the background.

in the *ABS Record* provided the basis for identifying operational failures of crucial items such as anchoring systems and tailshafts, prompting detailed research and specific Rule changes. In 1979, ABS began offering its computerized online survey status programs to the marine industry. With this system, owners of ABS-classed vessels worldwide gained direct access to the ABS database. With a terminal in his office, a fleet owner could obtain the survey particulars for each of his vessels at any time of day or night, anywhere in the world.

Six years later, the EAGLE system of computer software was released, bringing with it programs to calculate hull girder strength, structural properties, ship hydrostatics and stability, among other factors critical to design and construction. The program saved both time and money, by eliminating duplication of effort by the designer and ABS, as well as the reduction of paper flow and the delays involved in plan review.

With the installation of computers in ABS offices throughout the world, ABS engineers and surveyors could run programs on their own systems, eliminating the expense of connecting with the mainframe computers at headquarters. EAGLE programs were also available under a licensing arrangement to shipyards and designers. ≋

tasks on an outside time-shared system. With the creation of ABSCOMP, all of these calculations could be done within ABS. But ABSCOMP was not restricted to ABS alone. Its technical programs and data processing services were also offered to industry.

Other initiatives included the ABS Information Retrieval System (ABSIRS), a data bank that contained all information

1975

THE CHILL WINDS OF RECESSION

Activity in manned submersible units was on the increase in the mid-1970s, as the offshore oil industry pushed into depths where conventionally-equipped human divers could only function for limited periods. ABS classed three new units in 1975, raising to 31 the total listed in the *ABS Record*. But when the year ended, 26 manned submersibles were being built according to requirements spelled out in the ABS *Guide for Classification of Manned Submersibles*, the first such published.

The Guide had been first published in 1968, with the 48-foot long submersible *BEN FRANKLIN* as the first submersible built to ABS class. With a 252-day life-support system, this underwater vessel carried a crew of six on an expedition along the Gulf Stream. As commercial enterprise began calling for the dexterity of human hands to perform lengthy jobs at depths of 1,000 feet, less esoteric tasks awaited these technologically advanced craft.

PC 1204, a manned submersible earmarked for use in the North Sea, was one of 41 classed by ABS or being built to class with operating depths of 1,000 feet or more.

ABS took on the job of establishing standards for shipboard decompression chambers for the divers, as well as the submersible diving bells that moved divers between the deck of a mother ship and the sea floor. By the end of the decade, ABS had developed and issued comprehensive *Rules for Building and Classing Underwater Systems and Vehicles* to provide guidance for the designers and builders of these craft.

Later generations of remotely operated vehicles (ROVs), capable of carrying tools for cutting, cleaning and a multiplicity of other tasks required for such deepwater jobs as inspection and repair, continue in service. Hundreds of such vehicles operated electronically from their mother ships are currently in use, many classed to ABS standards.

The 169-foot long POINT CONCEPTION plies through the waters on missions as a tugboat, or supply vessel, at speeds up to 12 knots.

Although ABS classed more than 2,000 new vessels, and reviewed a record 51,300 hull plans, during 1975 there were some signs of slackening in the number of new ship contracts being placed. Orders indicated a switch of emphasis by owners to small vessels, such as tugs and offshore supply boats, from the tankers that had been dominating orderbooks. Many of the vessels for which ABS reviewed plans did not reach the building dock as the chill winds of an economic slowdown began to brush the maritime industry.

But there were positive elements. The ABS order backlog remained strong; signposting continued fleet growth in the short term. There was renewed interest in maritime applications of aluminum, prompting ABS to issue *Rules for Building and Classing Aluminum Vessels*, the first such standards to be published by any classification society.

In contrast to the earlier application of aluminum within the superstructure of the large passenger liners, the new Rules covered classification requirements for the design and survey of all-aluminum vessels 100 to 500 feet in length. Over the next 20 years, large numbers of groundbreaking, high speed craft, from hydrofoils to wave-piercing catamarans would be constructed using the standards contained in these Rules. ≋

1976

Another form of service to industry undertaken at this time by ABS, in concert with the US Maritime Administration (MARAD), was a long-term investigation to determine the limitations on the use of electroslag and electrogas welding. New flux-cored electrodes were coupled with lower heat input rates and faster travel speeds. Preliminary test results using these techniques looked encouraging – but a follow-up study was needed.

This materials research project was one of many inquiries ABS conducted in association with government or industry to find new methods, materials, systems or Rules that would improve safety within the marine industry.

Technical participation in the development of standards for Safety of Life at Sea (SOLAS), load line, and tonnage certification were other contributions that ABS offered to the maritime industry. ABS was authorized to conduct surveys

and issue SOLAS Certificates for 46 governments, and 70 governments granted the society permission to conduct surveys and issue Load Line Certificates. ABS also issued National Tonnage Certificates on behalf of 36 governments, as well as for the Suez and Panama Canals. ≋

1978

GROWTH PROMPTS MOVE TO BIGGER HEADQUARTERS

ABS passed an historic milestone in 1977 with the classification of over 100 million gross tons of shipping. This was accomplished when 1,655 new vessels were accepted into class during the year raising the fleet total to 14,884 vessels totaling just over 102 million gross tons.

During this prolonged burst of shipbuilding activity, new performance records were being set by ABS. In 1978, the society recorded more than 15,000 vessels in class, finally reaching an all-time high of 15,837 vessels in 1980. In 1979, the aggregate fleet size broached 109 million gross tons, reaching a record 109.4 million gt in 1981 and representing a more than 100 percent increase in fleet size in just 10 years. The previous year had seen the establishment of the record dead-weight tonnage under ABS class at just over 196 million tons.

With an oversupply of tonnage plaguing virtually every sector, these figures were to prove high water marks not to be attained again before the turn of the century.

Planning for the future, ABS consolidated all headquarters and subsidiary operations in a larger building at 65 Broadway in New York City.

Of equal importance, this surge in activity had created a need to expand the ABS headquarters in New York. ABS was already leasing five floors of additional office space in nearby buildings. By purchasing a 21-story building at 65 Broadway in New York City, the ABS headquarters and its subsidiaries, ABSCOMP and ABSTECH, were consolidated in one location by the end of 1978.

The 33,000-ton MOLIKPAQ is a caisson submersible unit built in an all-steel hull that allows it to drill in the Arctic for the entire year and, when its work is completed, to be moved to another location.

NEW OCEAN ENGINEERING DIVISION ESTABLISHED

This extreme pace of new ship construction was matched by a comparable level of activity in the offshore industry. One reason for the rapid ABS expansion was its recognition as the preferred classification society for mobile offshore drilling units (MODUs). As more of these units were classed, ABS was handling nearly two-thirds, or 243 units, of the worldwide fleet including many units in the North Sea following the society's recognition as a certification authority by the UK Department of Energy.

In response, a new ABS Division was established in 1978 to deal specifically with the fixed, or site-specific offshore structures. The new Division's Offshore Structures department concentrated on six areas: documentation and certification; steel structures; concrete structures; environment and foundations; instrumentation, machinery and electrical; and inspection. The Research and Development department was also incorporated into the new Division.

The newly established Division was promptly selected by the US government to develop a set of *Requirements for Verifying the Structural Integrity of Outer Continental Shelf Platforms for the United States Geological Survey*. The results of this project formed the basis of governmental regulations on fixed offshore structures drilling for oil and gas on the outer US Continental Shelf. In a related development, seven governments granted ABS the authority to certify platform structures installed off their shores.

ABS' efforts to maintain a close association with the offshore oil and gas industry led to a further technical reorganization late in 1984 that brought together all the expertise from ABS departments dealing with the increasingly sophisticated mobile offshore drilling units and fixed offshore structures. The new division was also given total responsibility for plan review, structural analysis, and quality assurance monitoring during the course of construction, as well as all periodic surveys. ≋

WILLIAM N. JOHNSTON

President: 1977-1979
President and Chairman: 1979-1986

1979

EXPANDED RULEMAKING

From the initial issuance of a single publication containing *Rules for the Surveying and Classing of Wooden Vessels* in 1870, the range and scope of ABS' technical standards had expanded dramatically. Yet the department responsible for new Rule development, as well as the updating of existing Rules, was and remains a part of ABS that is often overlooked. As the backbone of the classification society, this work is never ending.

An ABS surveyor inspects the prototype of a container before it receives the ABS certification seal.

The new Rules published by ABS in 1979 alone included: *Guide for Ships Burning Coal*; *Guide for Building and Classing Industrial Systems*; *Guide for Building and Classing Offshore Racing Yachts*; and *Guidance Manual for Material Selection and Inspection of Inert Gas Systems*. Revised or updated Rules included: *Rules for Building and Classing Mobile Offshore Drilling Units*; *Rules for Building and Classing Steel Vessels for Service on Rivers and Intracoastal Waterways*; and *Guide for Repair and Cladding of Shafts*.

Also, an edition of the *Rules for Building and Classing Steel Vessels* was published in an eighth language – Italian.

Over the next 20 years this list would continue to expand until more than 60 Rules, Guides and technical Advisory Notes would be available to industry by the end of the century. By this time the primary *Steel Vessel Rules* would have grown to almost 4,000 pages in length and be available electronically on CD-Rom. ≋

1980

WORLD'S LARGEST MERCHANT SHIP CLASSED BY ABS

A 1,504-foot tanker, the world's largest merchant ship, was built to ABS class in 1980. The vessel was to retain this title throughout its life as changing economies dictated greater efficiencies from smaller tankers in the 250-300,000 dwt range. Appropriately named *SEAWISE GIANT*, this 564,763 deadweight ton vessel was owned by the C.Y. Tung Group of Companies in Hong Kong.

Equally impressive, ABS classed the world's largest mobile offshore derrick-barge in 1985, a column-stabilized unit owned by McDermott Inc. The unit measured 625 feet by 322 feet by 165 feet and was used for heavy-lift offshore construction work. Two onboard cranes provided a combined lift capacity of 13,200 short tons. ≋

SEAWISE GIANT, launched in 1979, was "jumboized" from 1,237 to 1,504 feet, 50 feet longer than the Sears Building in Chicago, the then world's tallest.

1981

ABS has always enjoyed a special relationship with the US government in recognition of the unique technical capabilities and impartiality of the Bureau and its worldwide staff of surveyors and engineers. This global ABS network of technical expertise and experienced manpower is viewed as an efficient, economical method for government agencies to conserve resources while maintaining high standards of performance.

The early 1980s saw a formalization of what had been a largely ad hoc working arrangement through the signing of two important Memorandums of Understanding with the US Coast Guard.

The first of these granted authority to ABS to issue ad-measurement and tonnage certificates for all US-flagged vessels on behalf of the Coast Guard. The second, and more comprehensive MOU, provided for Coast Guard acceptance of ABS plan review and approval of the hull structure and machinery of ships,

After its construction to ABS class in 1981, the WILLIAM J. DELANCEY was the largest ship on the Great Lakes. The 68,060-dwt vessel was more than 1,000 feet long and had a beam of 105 feet.

mobile offshore drilling units and barges classed by the society, as well as crude oil washing systems and certain piping systems.

This period also saw a burgeoning relationship forming between the Bureau and the US Navy as ABS began to develop specifications for hull steel requirements and designations for use by the military. An early project saw ABS class a series of 240-foot-long salvage vessels for the Navy, working with them on the application of Rules and specifications to non-combatant ships.

It was not long before ABS provided a more formalized structure for working with the US government with the creation of a Government Services Unit. Among the government agencies targeted were the Maritime Administration, the Army Corps of Engineers, the United States Coast Guard, the Military Sealift Command, Naval Sea Systems Command, Customs Service and National Oceanographic Administration.

The result of such cooperation was evidenced in the delivery of the first maritime prepositioning ship, *2ND LT. JOHN P. BOBO*, to the US Navy in 1985. It was one of 13 such vessels designed to support the rapid deployment of US forces and military equipment worldwide. Five of this initial series of

ships were built; eight more were created by extensive conversions of existing commercial ships, including the unique series of very fast Sea-Land containerships that had been delivered in 1969.

It provided the genesis of a program that was to continue through into the early part of the next century. The benefits of such flexible, rapid response, military support vessels were recognized with an increasingly ambitious newbuilding program, in which ABS played an extensive role, largely split between Avondale Industries of New Orleans and NASSCO of San Diego. ≈

2ND LT. JOHN P. BOBO, operated by the Military Sealift Command, loaded with vehicles and supplies provided Marine Corps operations with logistical support.

1982

INTRODUCING QUALITY ASSURANCE

By now the worldwide recession, coupled with the aftershocks of the ambitious newbuilding program of the 1970s were beginning to have serious consequences for the international shipping industry. The initial impact on ABS was softened due to the length of its new construction backlog, yet the organization continued to aggressively seek ways to provide enhanced services to its clients, while initiating internal efficiencies.

A particular focus was the ABS program by which the quality of various materials and equipment used on board an ABS classed vessel was assessed. Ten plants manufacturing a variety of products joined the ABS Quality Assurance Program in 1982. At year's end there were 80 such manufacturing plants worldwide.

Under this program, ABS representatives scrutinized a company's various manufacturing processes. A firm that

The six-story ABS House was opened in January 1982 on London's Frying Pan Alley, and serves as the organization's European headquarters.

satisfied the yearly on-site plant audit was issued an ABS Certificate of Manufacture. The program was an innovative precursor to the quality management systems introduced by the International Standards Organization such as the ISO 9000 standard. A future ABS affiliate, ABS Quality Evaluations was to become a global leader in auditing to these standards and ABS itself would be the first classification society to meet these new internationally-accepted quality standards.

Scenes from the assembly line at MTU, Friedrichshafen, Germany, show the cleanliness, order and precision hand assembly that characterize the workshops of leading marine diesel engine manufacturers.

During this period of development, ABS had 14 programs covering the building of diesel engines, container refrigeration machinery, reduction gears, and rolled steel products. A product line could be submitted for approval according to ABS' established Rules and standards. If accepted, ABS would issue a Type Approval Certificate to the company and add the product to the ABS List of Approved Equipment.

Recording rapid growth, more than 700 industrial plants involved with a broad range of products and processes had enrolled in, and met the criteria of one of the many ABS quality assurance programs by the end of the decade. At that time ABS established an internal quality assurance program to monitor its own exclusive services, with particular attention given to vital ship components and functions.

While this formalized the network of independent programs already in use, it also added new ones, such as quality audits of ABS services and procedures. It also served to reemphasize the critical importance of service to clients in all ABS activities. ≋

1983

MODUs FOR THE ARCTIC

The offshore industry continued to embrace ingenious technical solutions to the seemingly impossible challenge of cost effectively extracting oil from the most hostile environments. Nothing better illustrated this than developments undertaken in the bleak Beaufort Sea area of the Arctic. ABS worked in tandem with pioneers who were breaching these new technological frontiers with the development of mobile caisson submersible drilling units able to operate year round in the heavy pack ice.

A four-part caisson drilling unit, GLOMAR BEAUFORT SEA I was the first of its kind designed to work in Arctic waters. The concrete island drilling unit stands atop an all-welded steel base of 312 by 295 feet divided into two water-tight compartments.

Prior to their development, the number of drilling days in the Beaufort Sea area, using more conventional drillships supported by icebreakers, was limited to about 100 days. The huge floating caisson units, with a square deck size often exceeding the length of a football field, could ballast down and sit on the sea bottom. Constructed of either all steel, or a combination of steel and concrete, these impregnable units were able to resist the extreme pressures of the ice.

The role of ABS within such projects reinforced the society's position as the acknowledged leader in MODU and offshore classification. In 1983 ABS had 525 MODUs in class and had experienced a 100 percent increase in new construction activity over the previous year.

By 1985 this number had grown to 574, or two-thirds of the MODUs classed by all societies, prompting the release of new *Rules for Mobile Offshore Drilling Units*, which better defined ABS practices for approving jacking systems for self-elevating drill rigs and for ballast systems for column-stabilized units. ≋

Operating at a depth of 203 feet, this platform was the first of three ABS-classed offshore structures installed in the Gulf of Thailand during 1983.

1984

DIVERSIFICATION CONTINUES

The mid-1980s saw ABS diversifying, through its affiliated companies, to counter the prolonged slump afflicting the international shipping industry. In 1983, ABSTECH registered with the World Bank and eight other development banks to become a recognized industrial consultant with the United Nations Industrial Development Organization.

ABSTECH, on behalf of the Sebring Utilities Commission, provided owners representation, quality control, and progress reports during the construction of a 40,000 KW diesel power plant.

Also in 1983, the affiliate, ABS/Boiler and Marine Insurance Company (ABS/BMIC), provided underwriting and financial services. It soon became apparent, however, that substantial contributions could be made in the field of boiler and pressure vessel inspection.

Consequently, in 1984, another affiliate, the ABS/BMIC Boiler and Pressure Vessel Division was established and received authorization by the National Board of Boiler and Pressure Vessel Inspectors to carry out examinations of boilers, pressure vessels and pressure-related equipment according to the Code of the American Society of Mechanical Engineers (ASME).

ABSTECH offered another service to the maritime industry in 1983 – Fuel Oil Testing.

Shipowners seeking confirmation that bunkers taken on board met specified chemical characteristics could air courier samples to an ABS Test Laboratory in the United States. After performing analytical tests, the results were sent by telex to the ship operator with appropriate recommendations for treatment. ≋

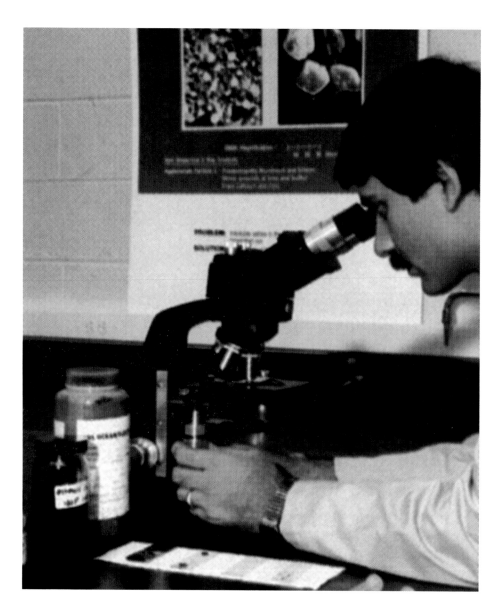

A microscope is employed using the ABS Oil Testing Service Program to identify solid contaminants that could damage an engine by plugging fuel filters and nozzles.

1985

ONE MILLION CONTAINERS

Throughout the 1970s and 1980s the ABS container certification program experienced continuous strong growth, reflecting the rapid acceptance internationally of this method of handling an ever widening range of commodities. In 1975 the program passed the 225,000 milestone, with another 37,200 units on order. Just two years later this had surged to more than 100,000 containers on order. Within another two years the total number of ABS certified containers had passed the 500,000 mark.

The number of containers certified by ABS, including various dry cargo, open top, platform and thermal units, reached more than one million early in the third quarter of 1985.

By 1985, one million units were certified, and ABS issued a new section of its *Rules for Certification of Containers* to further extend their scope. Those requirements focused on certification of the container chassis – the wheeled, skeletal semi-trailer used to carry a container from the port by truck or rail to its ultimate destination. ≋

Double stacked trains provided a speedy, reliable and cost efficient distribution system for marine containers within North America.

1986

THE RECESSION BEGINS TO BITE

The combination of a global economic recession and massive oversupply of tonnage from the profligate building boom of the 1970s was proving calamitous to the international shipping industry. Shipbuilding activity remained lackluster with the world orderbook falling to its lowest level in 20 years. This, combined with ABS' traditional insistence on the most demanding standards of structural strength, significantly depressed the volume of tonnage entering the ABS classed fleet.

ABS broke with tradition and left New York City, by relocating the World Headquarters to a new, five-story office building in suburban Paramus, New Jersey.

This downturn was coupled with an accelerated pace of scrapping by owners struggling to cover even their operating costs during the prolonged slump in charter rates. More than 200 vessels a year, with a heavy preponderance of tankers, were leaving the ABS fleet as they headed to the scrap yard.

To cut costs and find adequate space for its operations, ABS moved its World Headquarters to Paramus, New Jersey, just across the Hudson River and minutes away from New York City where the

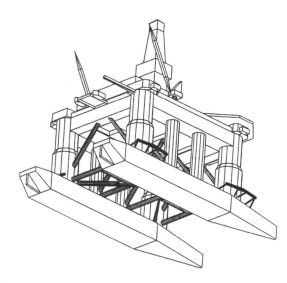

The stability of a semisubmersible drill rig design is checked by R&D engineers using graphic models.

society had been based for 123 years. The new five-story building was expected to increase business efficiency.

The move spurred a series of reorganizations that would, over the next five years, reshape the manner in which ABS operated. A preliminary step was the creation of the ABS Ship Engineering Department (SED), assigned to handle all classification, statutory and certification requirements of the conventional ship industry. SED responsibilities included hull and machinery plan review, as well as materials and manufacturing processes, quality assurance, container certification, and equipment type approval.

Recognizing the importance of Research and Development (R&D) to the marine and offshore industry, this ABS department was raised to a divisional status, allowing its engineers to work more closely with all sections of the classification society.

For example, programs developed by R&D to examine a ship structure's behavior were used to analyze the design of the world's then 12 largest containerships. The *AMERICAN NEW YORK* and 11 other containerships of the same class, built in South Korea to ABS class for US Lines, were 58,000 deadweight ton ships, each with a capacity of 4,238 20-foot equivalent unit containers.

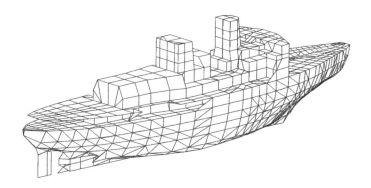

Data collected by the US Coast Guard icebreaker POLAR SEA, heavily instrumented to determine the force of ice ramming against the bow, helped naval architects design ships to move oil from offshore Arctic fields to world markets.

The 58,000 dwt AMERICAN NEW YORK, shown passing through the Panama Canal, was one of a series of the largest containerships delivered in the mid-1980s.

But more was needed. It had become clear to executive management that major new initiatives would be necessary if ABS was to maintain its leading position in promoting the safety of life and property. Therefore, the organization embarked on a major strategic plan, the purpose of which was to decentralize the organizational structure, to bring its classification and related services closer to clients around the world, and to allow more efficient operations. The plans were outlined to, and accepted by, the Board of Managers at their semiannual meeting in September 1986. Because of the magnitude of this undertaking, it was recognized that it would best be accomplished in two stages. ≋

RICHARD T. SOPER

President: 1986
President and Chairman: 1987-1990

1987

The first stage of the strategic plan was implemented at the outset of 1987: ABS operations worldwide were decentralized into ten regions, headed by regional managers. Each was staffed and supported as a business entity with responsibility for all the corporate operations in that region including ABS, ABSTECH, ABS/BMIC and ABS Government Services.

At the same time, most of the business functions were maintained at the Paramus, New Jersey headquarters, which also continued to serve as the support and control center. Also at headquarters, a Technical Services Group was formed, merging ship engineering, offshore engineering, R&D and regulatory affairs.

The year 1987 was an exceptional one for ABS. Not only did it mark a significant, redirection of the organizational structure and management practices to position the society for the next century, but it also marked the society's 125th

An ABS surveyor checks the engine console to verify tests of a vessel for unattended-engine room certification. By the end of 1987, there were 1,310 vessels with this designation classed by ABS.

The 590-foot GREEN LAKE, built by IHI Kure and owned by Central Gulf Lines, Inc., was one of 62 vehicle carriers in ABS class or in the ABS orderbook by the end of 1987.

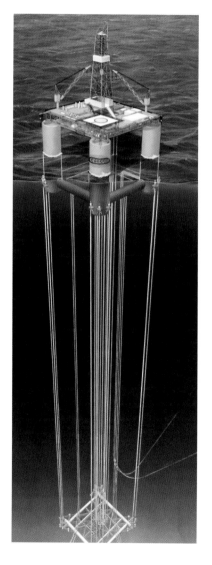

Anniversary. ABS could look back with pride on a period symbolizing a rich, progressive and unique history of promoting safety of life and property through certification, inspection, quality assurance, analysis and ship classification services.

At the end of its 125th Anniversary year, ABS had in its classification 13,172 vessels of 93,507,500 gross tons from 90 countries of registry. These figures emphasize the difficulties that the industry and the organization had been confronted with over the previous six years. It had been as recently as 1981 that fleet size had topped 109 million gross tons and reached almost 16,000 vessels.

Yet there were hopeful signs in the 701 vessels of over 4.6 million gt building or on order to be built to ABS classification as the year came to a close. And the offshore sector remained busy with particular emphasis on floating production and offloading systems for petroleum development from marginal and newly discovered fields. ABS was involved with such projects offshore Australia, China, Brazil, Yemen, Canada and the United States.

ABS was also engaged in several other significant offshore projects including fixed platform certification in the Persian Gulf, off Taiwan and in the waters of the Australian North West Shelf. Also offshore production systems in Canadian waters and the certification of a tension leg platform structure, the first such operational unit, in American waters.

By this time ABS was also authorized to conduct surveys and issue certificates for many governments in accordance with various international maritime conventions, specifically: 78 countries for Load Line; 75 for Tonnage Admeasurement; 59 for Safety of Life at Sea (SOLAS); and 36 for Marine Pollution (MARPOL). ≋

The 7,955-gt chemical carrier RACHEL B was built to ABS class and issued a certificate of fitness for the carriage of dangerous chemicals in bulk in accordance with the Code of the International Maritime Organization.

1988

TECHNICAL INNOVATIONS

Despite the weakness of the shipping market, this period was a time of intense technical development and innovation at ABS with projects covering a broad span of marine and offshore activity.

Many of these innovations were taking place in areas of small-vessel development, from submersibles to SWATH (small waterplane area twin hull) vessels.

In 1988 ABS supplied technical support services to the Naval Sea Systems Command for the design of its new SWATH-type research vessel *T-AGOS*. The previous year, Pacific Marine of Honolulu, Hawaii, asked ABS to class the first United States commercial SWATH vessel, an inter-island ferry named *NAVATEK I.*

The Ship Engineering Division approved designs for air-cushion vehicles, and 60-knot, water-planing, surface-effect ships, as well as unique hull types that were patented for superior sea-keeping ability and propulsive efficiency. ABS

Caribbean vacationers in photo at top enjoy breathtaking views of the ocean 150 feet below the surface in the ATLANTIS IV. The MARIEA III submersible (bottom) was built to ABS class by Oy Laivateollisuus AB. Through 1988, every tourist submersible built or being built since 1964 was classed by ABS.

VICTORIOUS, the US Navy's T-AGOS 19 SWATH surveillance vessel, under construction at McDermott Shipyard.

PRINCESA DACIL, a hydrofoil with a design speed of 43 knots, was built to ABS class by Kawasaki Heavy Industries Co. Ltd.

knowledge in these fields was incorporated in the *Rules for Building and Classing High Speed Craft.*

Engineers also reviewed the hull plans for racing yachts to be built with advanced composite plastics. ABS hull plan approval was a condition of entry for the prestigious around-the-world Whitbread Race.

There was growing interest in tourist submersibles, some of which carried as many as 50 people to a depth of 150 feet. A total of 66 submersibles of all types were in ABS class at the year's end. Additionally, all of the 19 tourist submersibles built or being built, starting with the *AUGUSTE PICCARD* in 1964, were ABS class.

But technical innovations extended far beyond small vessels. During 1988 five new American President Lines (APL) C-10 containerships, classed with ABS, were delivered by two West German shipyards, HDW and Bremer Vulkan. These were the first post-panamax containerships, their 39.4-meter beam

American President Lines' PRESIDENT POLK was one of five C-10 post-panamax ABS-classed containerships placed in service in 1988. Each had an original length of 853 feet, a beam of 129 feet, and a 4,340-TEU (20-foot equivalent unit) capacity.

made them too large to transit the Panama Canal, and provided a radical breakthrough in containership operation. When the shipyards needed to modify the structure of these 4,340 teu vessels for further lengthening, they relied on the finite element analyses performed by ABS.

In 1988 ABS was also involved in classing nine innovative refrigerated cargo vessels for the Del Monte Fruit Company,

built by Astilleros Espanoles in Spain, which included the latest thinking on refrigeration systems and cargo handling.

During the year, the Offshore Engineering Division (OED) received numerous inquiries related to new designs and conversions for: converting drilling units to production service; lengthening the legs of jackups; and reconfiguring jackups to cantilever configurations. In addition, numerous owners requested OED perform independent technical analyses of their projects with regard to class and regulatory matters.

The previous year the ABS MODU Stability Joint Industry Project (JIP) had been completed, significantly enhancing the knowledge required by government regulators to adequately assess additional stability requirements then being proposed for semisubmersible-type drilling units. The JIP was jointly funded by 17 participants representing all aspects of the offshore industry. These included designers and builders, drilling contractors, oil companies and government agencies. The ABS Research & Development Division and the ABS Offshore Engineering Division were the principal investigators and administrators of the project.

Two other major research programs dealing with the stability of semisubmersible offshore drilling units were being undertaken. On completion, the recommended criteria resulting from the ABS programs were implemented into the International Maritime Organization (IMO) MODU Code.

Such rapid advances in many fields posed challenges to ABS surveyors and engineers relative to engineering judgment, knowledge of the ever-changing government and statutory requirements and managerial skills. Consequently in 1989 the ABS training program was completely revamped and reorganized under a fulltime director of training responsible for developing seminars and educational programs for ABS surveyors and engineers worldwide. ≋

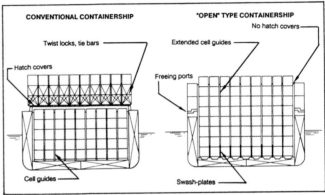

With the aid of in-house computer programs, ABS compiled proven methods for predicting water ingress into open hatch containerships based on seakeeping performance and supplemented by appropriate model testing.

EDYTH L, a 630-foot, 19,600-gt reefer container carrier built to ABS class for CRH Shipping Ltd., Hamilton, Bermuda.

1989

RAPID RESPONSE TEAM

The *EXXON VALDEZ* tanker casualty resulted in significant environmental pollution in Alaskan waters. As a result, in 1990 the United States Congress passed the Oil Pollution Act of 1990 (OPA90) – legislation that would impact the design, operation and liabilities associated with tank vessels. The law mandated double hulls for new tank vessels operating in US waters and provided for the phase-out of existing single hulled vessels over an extended period. ABS had extensive experience in classing double hull tankers and quickly prepared for an influx of orders for new vessels meeting OPA requirements.

Prior to the enactment of this new law, however, one of the most immediate impacts was to focus attention on how an owner responds in the critical early hours of a casualty to minimize loss and control pollution.

The ABSTECH Rapid Response Damage Assessment (RRDA) team provided around the clock service to shipowners.

Possessed of unique technical capabilities, ABS saw an opportunity to provide shipowners and offshore operators with immediate assistance to minimize casualty losses. Through its affiliate, ABSTECH, it formed a Rapid Response Damage Assessment team, on call 24-hours-a-day, comprised of skilled naval architects, engineers and former mariners. The concept was designed to expedite the emergency services that the organization had given the marine industry over the years.

Two levels of rapid response service were developed. The first was designed to provide clients with on-call review, analysis and consultation based on information that ABSTECH already had in-house on specific ships or offshore units. On the second level, clients supplied ABSTECH with additional information that enabled the organization's technical staff to calculate survivability, longitudinal strength, and damage and intact stability. With this data, ABSTECH used programs to create a model of the ship or offshore structure to provide fast advice.

This was a further example of the importance of ABSTECH's diversified activities to the ABS organization. The affiliate continued its growth pattern in both the marine and industrial sectors. Relative to the former – a wide range of assignments were completed worldwide, including condition surveys, inclining tests and stability studies, project management and on-site supervisory services, owner's representation, drawing and specification review and consultancy.

Relative to the latter – vendor inspections, especially in Europe, added to ABSTECH's leading position in crane-certification work. Its quality audit program with American Institute of Steel Construction grew to 176 plants enrolled by the year's end. In related work, the American Petroleum Institute and Steel Structures Paint Council contracted ABSTECH to assist them in similar programs. ≋

Third-party inspection was provided by ABSTECH on this 40-ton container crane built in Kilarney, Ireland, for the Dublin Port and Docks Board.

FRANK J. IAROSSI

President and Chairman: 1990-1993
Chairman: 1993-2004

1990

ABS 2000: A MAJOR REORGANIZATION UNDER A NEW CHAIRMAN

I n 1987 the American Bureau of Shipping had embarked on a strategic plan that resulted in a decentralization of the organizational structure. The purpose of the plan was to bring all ABS classification and related services, together with decision-making processes, closer to clients around the world. It was envisaged that this approach would not only enhance the quality of the services provided to clients but would also encourage more efficient operations. Because of the extent of this undertaking, it was to be accomplished in two stages. The first stage, implemented in 1987, involved the formation of ten regional business centers.

The second stage was outlined by newly appointed ABS Chairman Frank Iarossi in his mid-September 1990 presentation to the ABS Board of Managers, which approved the plan. Dubbed "ABS 2000" for its forward-looking approach, this reorganization had several strategic objectives:

BENJAMIN HARRISON was the first of two barge carriers built to ABS class at Avondale Shipyard and delivered to Waterman Steamship in 1990.

In 1990, a 133-foot midbody was added at the Jos. L. Meyer yard in Germany to the ABS-classed HOMERIC to create the 723-foot WESTERDAM for the Holland America Line.

- updating the management processes used to plan, allocate resources and monitor the performance of the enterprise;

- emphasizing the need for ABS to embrace the concepts of quality assurance in all its activities;

- undertaking a long-term, focused expansion of diversified non-marine services; and

- fostering employee participation, teamwork, leadership and excellence throughout the ABS organization.

- securing and enhancing long-term financial stability;

- decentralizing all routine technical, operational and administrative decision-making;

- establishing a streamlined executive office to focus on development of strategic plans and the establishment of goals, standards and policies;

- developing a dedicated marine research and development group coordinated from the executive level;

- emphasizing state-of-the-art technology in producing and delivering technical design analyses and engineering services;

The new ABS organization providing classification and marine-related services comprised a corporate office and three regional divisions. The divisions had authority, responsibility and accountability for all marine-related technical and operational activities within prescribed geographic areas, Europe, Pacific and the Americas. The corporate office,

The ABS corporate office was relocated to the 106th floor, Tower II, of New York City's World Trade Center in late 1991.

relocated back to New York City, had three components: an executive office, a marine research and development group, and a service center for clients.

Each marine-related division was fully self-supporting and managed as a business center. All three divisions followed the same management processes and reporting requirements and had the delegated authorities. Consistency throughout the divisions was assured through oversight at the corporate office.

ABS Europe was organized as an operating division of ABS with management responsibility for activities in Europe, Africa and the Middle East regions. Its main office was in London, with a regional office in Piraeus responsible for activities in the eastern Mediterranean, East Africa and Arabian Gulf regions.

ABS Pacific was organized as an operating division of ABS with management responsibilities for activities in Asia and Australasia. Its main office was located in Singapore, with a regional office in Yokohama responsible principally for activities in Japan, Korea, the Philippines and Taiwan.

ABS Americas was organized as an operating division of ABS with management responsibility for activities in North, Central and South America. Its principal office was located in Houston with a regional office in Rio de Janeiro responsible for all activities in Latin America.

The C.S. GLOBAL LINK (left) cablelaying ship and sister ship C.S. GLOBAL SENTINEL was built at Far East Levingston Shipbuilding Ltd. to ABS class for Transoceanic Cable Ship Co., Inc., an AT&T subsidiary. Each ship could carry 4,100 nautical miles of fiberoptic cable.

ABS Industrial Verification, Inc. was formed as a wholly owned, for-profit affiliate of ABS to provide advisory and verification services for engineering, construction and on-going operations in non-marine industries.

ABS Quality Evaluations, Inc. was formed as a for-profit affiliate of ABS to provide third-party assessment and certification of quality management systems to a wide range of quality standards, including the internationally sanctioned ISO 9000 series covering quality management system standards.

Another affiliate, ABS Boiler and Marine Insurance Company, continued to provide inspection services to the ASME pressure vessel code and assisted fabricating plants in obtaining the ASME stamp. It also provided related services to other recognized industry standards.

ABS Industrial Verification took on the non-marine services formerly provided by ABS Worldwide Technical Services, Inc. (ABSTECH). Non-classification marine work, formerly provided by ABSTECH that was of the not-for-profit type was now performed by ABS Marine Advisory Services (MAS), a department of the American Bureau of Shipping. In addition, a wholly owned affiliate of ABS, ABS Marine Services, Inc., was formed to provide for-profit marine services of the type formerly provided by ABSTECH, which was later dissolved.

The HSING MAY, a 705-foot, 36,438-gt bulk carrier, was built to ABS class in the People's Republic of China.

A number of further steps were implemented to enhance the role of technology. Four major decentralized technical groups were established in Houston, London, Singapore and Yokohama to direct all of the organization's engineering activities. Within the Houston technical group, two new functions were created: an advanced analysis section to focus on solutions to problems requiring complex or dynamic methodology, and a risk assessment section to focus on loss control techniques and to identify and reduce potential risks.

An additional element of the reorganization was the creation of four Technical Focus Groups covering tank vessels, passenger and cruise ships, offshore drilling units and

JOHN YOUNG, an 856-foot, 149,995-dwt oil carrier, was built to ABS class for Chevron Transportation Corporation by IHI, Kure, Japan.

liquefied gas carriers to make the technical expertise of ABS more readily available to the industry. Their purpose was to present the extensive capabilities of ABS at technical conferences, to extend the expertise in each area by assisting with R&D and various Rule development projects, and to provide additional expertise as needed to the three worldwide divisions.

A central element of the restructuring plan was to encourage continuous improvement in the manner in which ABS operated to forestall the need for subsequent major, unsettling reorganizations and to better control costs. Implementation of the reorganization began in the early part of 1991 and all the initial changes were in place and operating by early 1992. ≋

1991

HARNESSING COMPUTING POWER

In 1990, significant technological advancements were initiated as part of the ABS 2000 strategic plan. Perhaps the most noteworthy was the expansion from a centralized mainframe computer environment to one that introduced a global PC-based network as the main office computing tool.

BORAL GAS, a 2,300 cubic meter liquefied gas carrier, was built to ABS class for Boral Gas Ltd., with ABSTECH assisting in project management.

The network initially connected the New York, London, Singapore and Houston offices, but was steadily expanded to embrace the principal offices of ABS around the world. The goal was to establish an integrated PC-based network designed to handle all normal office functions and selected engineering functions.

But this renewed focus on computing power was not confined to ABS' own internal systems. By 1990 numerous advanced software programs were available from ABS to designers, builders and owners. Many were original programs developed by ABS, others involved refining and adding value to commercially available software. Wherever possible, ABS continued to design its software for cost-effective PCs and workstations rather than expensive mainframe systems.

One of the most noteworthy programs was OMSEC, a PC-based Optimization Midship Section Scantling Design Program based on the ABS *Rules for Building and Classing Steel Vessels*. This program was especially useful in the preliminary design of vessels such as tankers. It was a cost-effective tool for determining and validating the longitudinal strength members of a ship. Users selected an initial set of scantlings that satisfied the ABS Rules, the program then optimized the weight of the scantlings while maintaining the longitudinal bending stresses of the midship section as specified by the Rules.

This was quickly followed by the production of the *Steel Vessel Rules* on laser disk (CD-Rom), in addition to the 2,000-page printed volume. Laser disk technology allowed users to view the Rules on computer monitors quickly and easily. Another technology first was electronic plan review capability whereby documents could be electronically scanned into a system, allowing ABS engineers to make use of electronic overlays for noting comments and drawing amendments. Calculations, Rule requirements and related correspondence could all be viewed and linked through computer terminals. Annotated drawings could then be transmitted back to the submitter, either electronically or by hard copy. ≋

The self-elevating drilling unit SAGAR UDAY was built to ABS class for the Oil and Gas Commission of India.

1992

This early part of the new decade proved challenging for ABS within the market. Despite a steady inflow of newly-built vessels, the society continued to experience a net loss of tonnage. By the end of 1991 the fleet had dipped to 91.28 million gross tons and 13,172 vessels.

Clearly the recently established strategic objectives of gaining financial self-sufficiency, by increasing the organization's share of the newbuilding market and improving operating efficiencies, were assuming overriding importance. It was reasoned that a key to achieving these targets was for ABS to be recognized as the leader in marine technology.

To this end a series of initiatives were undertaken that would soon transform the manner in which classification standards were established. The first of these was the Dynamic Loading Approach (DLA) – a design-by-analysis procedure for more accurate modeling of expected ship loads and dynamic stresses than with traditional methods. DLA allows a more

SCARABEO 5, a column-stabilized drilling unit, with a length of 366 feet, a width of 237 feet and a height of 124 feet, was ABS classed. The unit was built by Fincantieri, Navali Italiani S.p.A.

rational distribution of material in the hull structure and results in conservatively-biased scantlings. DLA quickly received widespread acceptance and was soon being applied to analyses of tankers, container carriers and LNG vessels.

The 25,000-gt, 772-passenger, cruise ship COSTA MARINA is shown following its conversion from a containership.

The next step was the pioneering development known as RULES 2000. The objective of the program was to improve ship safety through the use of advanced technology. This was to be achieved through the modernization of ABS Rules using state-of-the-art analytical techniques, development of advanced design resources and technical support services.

A second phase of RULES 2000 was an ambitious undertaking, parallel to DLA, to enhance the applicability of traditional ABS hull-structure requirements through the development of strength criteria for all large commercial vessels based on a first-principles engineering approach. This revolutionary, dynamic-based approach to the design and evaluation of ship structures was named ABS SafeHull.

SafeHull would prove to be the most significant technical development to advance the analysis of hull structures in the history of ABS. It was also the most ambitious and expensive investment in new technology ever undertaken by the society, requiring two years of intense development prior to its initial release to the marine industry in September 1993. That initial release was applicable to new tankers. It was quickly followed by an updated version that also allowed for the structural assessment of existing tankers.

In applying SafeHull, the loads and stresses imposed on a hull structure, for the first time, could be quantified in an integrated and realistic manner. SafeHull provided an innovative, flexible approach that considered corrosion as well as the dominant failure modes – yielding, buckling and fatigue. By adapting SafeHull to existing vessels, ABS also reached another milestone by developing services to identify critical areas, thereby allowing enhancements to be made as appropriate.

With the passage of time and the gathering of practical service histories the value of the ABS SafeHull System was clearly validated. Ships designed to SafeHull criteria were demonstrably stronger and therefore deemed more robust ships. Shipowners quickly recognized this as not only a responsible goal, but also one that made logical business sense since more durable structures are less susceptible to failure and require less repair.

Development of the SafeHull system continued so that a version addressing bulk carriers could be released in 1994, a version for containerships in 1996, for floating production,

storage and offloading (FPSO) vessels in 2000, and for liquefied natural gas carriers (LNG) in 2004.

In extending SafeHull's application from tankers to bulk carriers and other ship types, ABS engineers, mindful of the structural differences, identified particular structural areas and conditions warranting special consideration. These findings were factored into the new versions and also formed the basis of recommendations proposed at a series of industry presentations and seminars that led to cooperative efforts within IACS, and with other industry groups throughout the 1990s, focused on addressing the issue of improving bulk carrier structural safety.

The ABS SafeHull System was conceived as a complete technical resource comprising two criteria – the *Guide for Dynamic-Based Design and Structural Evaluation* and the *Guide for Fatigue Assessment* – as well as a comprehensive suite of software applications programs, technical support services, related technical documentation and guidance.

As further testimony to the industry's regard for SafeHull, it garnered for ABS the prestigious 1994 Seatrade Award "for technical improvements leading to the reduction of risk to human life at sea." ≋

1993

BULK CARRIER SAFETY

From time to time the international shipping industry is confronted by a major safety issue that demands a concerted response from classification societies, legislators and owner's associations. It happened in the 1970s when several large tankers suffered catastrophic explosions while conducting routine gas freeing of the cargo spaces. A wide-ranging investigation of the causes led to the introduction of inert gas requirements for these vessels, eradicating the danger.

PACIFIC BRILLIANCE, a 36,438 dwt bulk carrier built in Jiangnan Shipyard in the People's Republic of China, was delivered in August 1993.

In the 1990s the industry found itself facing a similar dilemma as it became apparent that a growing number of older bulk carriers were disappearing without a trace while on loaded passage. The speed with which these vessels sank, taking all-hands with them, was not only a matter of gravest concern but it also left the industry with little tangible evidence from which to begin the analysis.

ABS took a leading role in the investigation into this issue. Before a complete explanation could be developed, ABS together with the other members of the International Association of Classification Societies (IACS), introduced a program establishing enhanced survey requirements for older bulk carriers and tankers. The objective was to more readily identify wasted vessel structural components, encouraging more prompt and thorough repairs. These enhanced surveys required arm's length visual inspection of the critical areas of the hull structure sufficiently cleaned to inspect coatings and detect possible cracking and deterioration in the steel or welds.

There was an identifiable improvement in the loss statistics once the more stringent requirements took effect. But it was recognized that these enhanced inspection requirements were only a first step towards solving the mystery. Fortuitously, a small number of bulk carriers suffered major structural failure yet survived, providing strong evidence for the investigation.

With time and a great deal of effort jointly expended by the survey and research sections of the principal classification societies, including ABS, a rational explanation for the failures was developed. Unfortunately more than 70 bulk carriers were lost and more than 700 seafarers went to a premature and watery grave before concrete proposals were put forward by industry to minimize the risk to which these vessels were exposed.

The analysis concluded that older bulk carriers, loaded with high density cargoes such as iron ore, particularly loaded in the favored alternate hold configuration, were at greatest risk. The determined fatal sequence of events involved the gradual detachment of a section of shell plating from the frames in either of the two foremost holds due to excessive corrosion or fatigue. The unsupported shell plating would finally crack and detach, immediately flooding the hold. Given the particular type of cargo and loading arrangement, the ingress of water placed too great a strain on the bulkheads and the supporting floors causing the sudden collapse of these structures, the rapid flooding of the adjacent holds and sinking of the ship.

The unraveling of this catastrophic mystery was a triumph of technical analysis. The unique capabilities of ABS SafeHull made a major contribution to that analysis and in the development of specific structural requirements, proposed by IMO and implemented by the class societies, that provided the necessary strengthening of the structure of existing vessels and amended the Rules for new construction.

These new requirements imposed a cost burden upon owners of existing vessels, many of whom opposed them. To those who issued criticisms, ABS senior management presented forceful rebuttals at major industry gatherings. ≋

1994

A COMMITMENT TO QUALITY

While the elements of ABS 2000 included many particular technical, managerial and administrative objectives, a central theme was an emphasis on quality and quality management in all aspects of ABS activities.

ABS was determined to become a model of quality management for other companies. Consistent with this all-encompassing objective, in 1992, ABS embarked upon a Total Quality Management (TQM) process.

A significant achievement for ABS in 1994 was its certification to the ISO 9001 standard, the first classification society to do so and one of the first global organizations. It represented a significant milestone in ABS' TQM journey. That all operating and support procedures worldwide had to be documented and conform to the requirements of this standard demonstrated the breadth of this undertaking.

The affiliated company, ABS Quality Evaluations, was also making significant progress in securing a prominent market position as a leader among ISO 9000 registrars. To this end, ABS QE received accreditation from Boards in the United States (RAB) and Holland (RvA), making it the first registrar to hold both United States and European accreditations.

IMPLEMENTING THE ISM CODE

As the clear benefits of safety and quality management systems began to be appreciated by both governments and industry, the IMO looked to the ISO model in preparing new safety standards for the international shipping industry. The International Safety Management Code (ISM Code) was adopted by the IMO in late 1993. Its purpose, when blandly stated as being to provide an international standard for the safe management and operation of ships and for pollution prevention, sounded no different to previous international safety initiatives. But it was the manner in which the ISM Code addressed this purpose that represented a radical new direction in safety standards.

Until the introduction of the Code, regulators had always relied on prescriptive rule making, specifically quantifying the safety equipment that was to be fitted on ships depending upon their size and cargo. The ISM Code approached safety from a management system perspective. It recognized that a company that operated in conformance with a recognized quality system would, inherently,

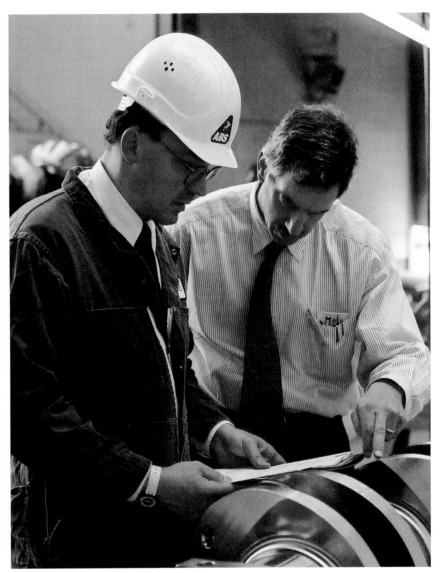

As part of ABS' commitment to continuous improvement, audits may be conducted to review survey procedures by any one of several auditing bodies or by one of ABS' own auditors.

operate more safely. The Code thus extended the concept of ship safety directly into the administrative functions of the company on shore.

ISM Certificates of Compliance were required by both the management company and each individual ship. A two-stage phase-in of these new requirements was announced, giving the industry more than three years to prepare before the highest risk vessels, such as tankers and passenger vessels, would have to comply. The requirement was met with puzzlement from many shipowners who found it difficult to grasp the implications of this completely new approach.

ABS promptly took steps to ease the adoption of the ISM Code's requirements for owners. It quickly put together training courses that explained the requirements and provided clear guidelines on how to implement a safety and quality management system that were presented in major shipping centers around the world. And ABS began to build and train a worldwide team of experienced personnel able to conduct the certifying audits. ABS, in conjunction with ABS QE, also developed a linked ISO 9000 quality management and ISM safety management program that was offered to owners seeking to demonstrate their commitment to the highest standards.

After an inordinate amount of industry-wide debate, the first phase of the Code took effect in July 1998 with much fanfare but little disruption, providing the foundation on which ship management systems of the future would be built. ≋

ABS surveyors, acting in a statutory capacity, may check safety equipment on board vessels.

1995

WORKING WITH THE US COAST GUARD

Early in 1995, ABS signed another Memorandum of Understanding with the US Coast Guard, expanding the scope of plan review and inspection procedures delegated to ABS. This MOU was to form the foundation of the Alternative Compliance Program, established in 1997 to reduce the duplication of tasks performed by the two organizations for verifying conformance of US-flag vessels in ABS class to required government safety standards.

The MOU also permitted ABS to conduct tonnage measurements of US-flag ships on behalf of the Coast Guard in accordance with the International Tonnage Convention of 1969. Building on this successful relationship, at mid-year the Coast Guard also authorized ABS to approve lifesaving, fire-protection and pollution prevention equipment required to be placed on commercial vessels in US waters. ≋

Mobil Oil's AMERICAN PROGRESS, a 45,367 dwt product carrier, entered the ACP on delivery in 1997.

1996

ABS SAFENET INTRODUCED

What was to become a landmark in the history of ABS occurred in late 1996 with the introduction of ABS SafeNet, a revolutionary life cycle fleet management and information network. SafeNet was designed as a cost-effective and easy-to-use system to assist shipowners and operators with the increasingly complex task of efficiently managing classification related information for their vessels.

The first phase of SafeNet provided direct, remote electronic access to the ABS Survey Status database by an owner for each ABS-classed vessel in that owner's fleet. It also contained a number of handy reference sources, such as a directory of ABS survey offices, a list of ABS Type Approved equipment, a directory of shipbuilding and repair facilities, and Port and flag State contacts.

Intensive development work continued throughout the year on a second, much more ambitious phase of ABS SafeNet.

This second phase was conceived to elevate the ship management capabilities to a new dimension, linking the survey status of a vessel to an owner's planned maintenance system for both hull and machinery. Specific modules were developed for the life cycle storage of complete condition assessment information, including gaugings, a structural history, vessel drawings, digitized condition photographs and machinery planned maintenance interfaces.

It soon became apparent that the benefit of SafeNet to shipowners would be enhanced if a wider, yet fully integrated

Owners are able to access the survey status on their vessels via ABS SafeNet.

suite of fleet management programs could be offered. As a consequence ABS Infolink, a subsidiary of the ABS Group of Companies, entered into a majority-owned joint venture with Nautical Technology Corp. (NTC) of New York in 1998. This venture, named ABS Nautical Systems LLC, was able to offer industry the most complete fleet management package available at the time, ranging from the technical complexity of the hull planned maintenance module to the practical usefulness of a crew payroll program, and purchasing and inventory control. ≋

1997

THE HUMAN ELEMENT

An increased awareness of the role the human element plays in marine safety ushered in a period when the traditional role of class was to expand, adding the subjective assessments of management systems (under the ISM Code) to the traditional engineering-based responsibilities of Rule development, design review and structural assessment.

But the issue raised broader questions. It was widely accepted that as many as 80 percent of all accidents could be traced to human error. In land-based industries there was growing acceptance of the role that ergonomics can play in determining the effectiveness of an operator's performance. Drawing on much of the research that had been undertaken in this field, ABS launched an important new study into the interaction of man and machine within the marine environment in 1993. The goal was

Each year more than 700 employees and contract surveyors attend ABS Academy training courses.

to provide guidance for improved designs of both equipment and the workplace that could help minimize the likelihood of human error and its harmful effects.

This represented the first effort by any class society to focus on the role that human factors engineering plays within marine safety. It led to the publication of the first ever guidance notes on the subject in 1997 to be followed shortly thereafter with equally groundbreaking standards for crew habitability on all ships and for the comfort of passengers on cruise ships and ferries.

But ABS also recognized that its own single greatest attribute lay with its worldwide staff of experienced surveyors and engineers. To promote consistently high standards, the ABS Academy opened in Houston in 1993. The formal training facility provided employees, from new hires to experienced surveyors, with the knowledge and skills needed to achieve the goal of continuous performance improvement. ≋

Mentoring and monitoring – experienced surveyors work alongside new hires providing training onsite.

1998

SAFETY, QUALITY, THE ENVIRONMENT

ABS QE was among the earliest organizations to attain accreditation as an ISO 14000 registrar when it was approved in 1996. Subsequently ABS developed a companion ISO 14000 environmental systems certification program for the marine industry.

ABS took the generic ISO standards and adapted them to marine operations, creating specific marinized standards for safety, quality and environmental management systems and formal SQE notations for owners. In 1998 the largest Greek shipowner, Ceres Hellenic Shipping Enterprises was the first operator of ABS-classed vessels to achieve certification to all three standards.

At the same time ABS itself committed to gaining ISO 14000 environmental management system certification for its own worldwide operations. After more than a year of intensive preparation this was achieved in mid-2000.

ABS' experience with these quality and environ-mental management systems, its conformance with the International Association of Classification Societies (IACS) quali-

Ceres Hellenic Shipping Enterprises was the first operator to achieve SQE certification from ABS.

ty system, and its commitment to the concept of continuous improvement convinced its management that these standards were the three cornerstones of a much-needed safety culture for the international shipping industry.

For, despite the constantly improving safety record of the world's fleet, occasional widely publicized casualties, often involving pollution of the shorelines of densely populated areas, prompted calls for more stringent regulation of the shipping industry. ABS became an out-spoken industry leader emphasizing that a strong system of self regulation through the mechanism of classification remained the preferred alternative to more intrusive governmental control of the industry.

PORT STATE CONTROL

Many nations sought to strengthen the protection of their own waters, coastlines and harbors through more aggressive inspection of vessels calling at their ports. Such Port State Control (PSC), especially strong in Europe, the US, Canada and Australia quickly took hold with several regional memorandums of understanding being forged between governments. By targeting a certain percentage of all ships for inspection and developing matrices to identify the highest risk vessels for particular scrutiny, PSC became one of the primary weapons in the on-going fight to improve maritime safety.

With each passing year, the annual reports from the various regional MOUs and from the US Coast Guard verified the significant progress that was being made by the industry and by ABS towards improved standards as evidenced by declining detention rates.

ABS introduced several specific initiatives to improve survey procedures. These included a lead surveyor program to provide more oversight and direction to the ABS exclusive surveyor staff; a requirement that two surveyors jointly conduct the Safety Equipment Surveys on bulk carriers over 15 years of age; and a requirement that an ABS principal surveyor or surveyor-in-charge review SOLAS and Load Line reports on vessels 10 years of age and older. ≋

1999

ABS RELOCATES TO HOUSTON

In 1999, ABS relocated its corporate headquarters and all but two departments to Houston, Texas from its traditional home in downtown New York City where, for nearly 140 years, it had been a prominent member of the maritime community. The move was perhaps the most visible manifestation of the society's commitment to a more efficient operational structure.

Together with the relocation, ABS initiated an ambitious Global Enterprise Management System project, intended to significantly improve the organization's future administrative capabilities. This upgrade was undertaken in conjunction with the beginnings of a sweeping reform in the way ABS managed information. Work began on developing a way to integrate computers and the Internet into the surveyor's activities to enhance delivery of traditional survey services.

ABS Plaza in Houston became the new corporate headquarters for ABS and its affiliates in late 1999.

FPSOs were in demand to service new deepwater oil fields.

again exceeding 100 million gross tons, or 16 percent of the world fleet. More significantly, ABS again enjoyed the leading market share in new vessel construction, with 23 percent of all tonnage on order specified to ABS class.

ABS achieved a growing market share in every ship sector, enjoying particular success among tankers and very large containerships.

ABS also enjoyed increasing work with other vessel types from ferries and cruise ships to gas carriers and FPSOs. ABS had classed FPSOs since the earliest days of that technology at the close of the 1970s. Throughout the 1990s ABS continued to lead in classing FPSOs as well as drillships, mobile offshore drilling units (MODUs), semisubmersibles and offshore support vessels. The society also pioneered the classification of such developing production technologies as tension leg platforms and spars.

By end-1999 ABS was firmly entrenched as one of the world's preeminent classification societies, with the ABS-classed fleet

The 1990s brought ABS great trials and successes. By the end of the decade, ABS was able to stand tall as a financially sound and technically advanced organization, with a clear vision and purpose, a strong and stable management team and a continuing commitment to financial, operational and technical excellence. In addition, ABS had become known as an outspoken and innovative advocate of increasingly tougher safety standards for the maritime industry.

Several significant practical standards were also developed and released to industry during 1999. Typical of these were *Guidance Notes on the Prevention of Air Pollution from Ships* – the first such Guide to be issued that interpreted the new IMO emissions standards – and *Guidance Notes on the Application of Synthetic Rope to Offshore Mooring*, the most comprehensive standards that had been developed for that rapidly evolving sector.

ABS GROUP ENDS A DECADE OF GROWTH

During 1999, ABS Group concluded a decade-long transformation from its traditional focus on industrial verification and marine-related services into an industrial consultancy with a broad skill set including ISO certification, safety, quality and environmental (SQE) certification, asset integrity management and risk-related services. ≋

2000

CHALLENGE AND PROGRESS

ABS surveyors work alongside owner's representatives when inspecting hull repairs.

ABS began the year by forcefully proposing that more stringent survey standards be imposed upon aging vessels. As the year progressed ABS outlined a sweeping series of measures designed to tighten classification scrutiny of aging ships, particularly tankers, maintained an outspoken advocacy of increasingly stringent safety standards, and worked to lead the industry in a self-generated reform focused on responsible operational practices.

Risk and reliability remained a strong focus of research efforts for the maritime and offshore energy markets during 2000, with one notable long-term research project initiated that year dedicated to developing standards for reliability-centered maintenance. For the offshore energy market, ABS responded to the widening scope of client needs by creating an Offshore Project Development Team to coordinate worldwide services to the fast changing energy sector.

ABS SafeHull made its first crossover into the offshore energy market as well, when ABS introduced a new version of SafeHull specifically tailored to structural analysis of the floating production, storage and offloading vessel (FPSO). SafeHull for FPSOs was the first analytical program that provided a rigorous, site-specific, targeted structural analysis for these specialized vessels.

Notable publications throughout the year reflected on-going research into Rules development as well, with ABS issuing *Guidance Notes on Risk Assessment Applications for Marine and Offshore Oil & Gas Industries*, and new Guides for building and classing floating production installations and the facilities aboard them.

Other milestones of 2000 included issuance of the 1,000th Type Approval certification, and the completion of ABS' first survey under the certificate of inspection requirements of the US Coast Guard's Alternate Compliance Program (ACP) for mobile offshore drilling units. Type

Traditional jackups increased in size and complexity as they moved into more hostile environments.

129

Approval verifies that a product is consistently manufactured to an established specification. ACP allows ABS surveys to be accepted in lieu of certain Coast Guard inspections.

ABS extended its relationship with the US Navy throughout the year, offering assistance for the Navy's plan to adopt commercial standards for select vessel types.

This included formalizing the processes and procedures used in the survey and classification of the over 100 vessels in the fleet of the Military Sealift Command, through the signing of a comprehensive Memorandum of Understanding.

ABS GROUP BUILDS ITS SKILL SETS

Close liaison with the USCG is an essential element in effective Port State Control.

ABS Group undertook a number of notable marine-related projects in 2000. In Mexico, certification of the modernization of the Cantarell offshore oil field continued. In Brazil, the government contracted the ABS affiliate to establish a safety regime that would apply to all exploration and production units in Brazilian waters. Brazilian energy giant Petrobras also turned to the affiliate to develop a new, risk-based approach to inspection and maintenance of FPSOs.

Photo courtesy of Geraldo Falcão

The PETROBRAS 35 floating production offloading and storage facility was converted from an ABS classed tanker, the JOSE BONIFACIO.

As the tanker sector focused on improving practices and the quality of its fleet, the ABS affiliate expanded its widely respected tanker Condition Assessment Program whose rating system was viewed by industry as an indication of the quality of vessels within the world's aging tanker fleet. ≋

2001

TRAGEDY, HOPE AND OPPORTUNITY

In the eyes of history, all events of 2001 shrink when compared to the terrorist attacks of 11 September (9/11) on New York and Washington DC. ABS, which had relocated its small remaining New York staff from the 106th floor of World Trade Center Tower Two to the 91st floor of Tower One, was miraculously spared the full depth of the tragedy. The first jetliner struck Tower One just above the ABS office, and all 16 people present at that horrible moment were able to safely escape the skyscraper before its collapse.

For ABS as an organization, 2001 was, considering its shocks and challenges, one of the most successful years in its long history. In late October, the ABS-classed fleet reached 109.8 million gross tons, its largest ever. The previous record was 109.4 million, achieved in 1981 at the close of a tanker-building boom. ABS ended 2001 as the preferred society for tanker classification, classing 30 percent of

all tankers on order and 25 percent of the existing tanker fleet.

In December 2001, two years of criticism of the maritime industry culminated with the adoption by the Parliament and Council of the European Union (EU) of wide-ranging maritime legislation. Principally, the legislation contained directives aimed at bolstering existing Port State Control legislation; tightening procedures for authorizing and monitoring the performance of classification societies; and gradually phasing-out single-hull oil tankers from EU waters by 2015.

European legislation confirmed the need to renew the world's tanker fleet with double hull vessels.

The continuing evolution of ABS SafeHull produced SafeHull for LNG Carriers, which gave the industry its first sophisticated analytical tools for determining the dynamic loads on an LNG vessel's hull, assessing the ship's 40-year fatigue life, and analyzing the sloshing loads on partially filled membrane tanks.

ABS also worked with the US Naval Sea Systems Command (NAVSEA) to develop supplements to the ABS Rules for naval purposes, covering such areas as structures, materials, diesel engines and gas turbines. ABS also developed the Naval Vessel Certification Plan Approach, adapting commercial practices to military use, and applied this approach to vessels for the US Coast Guard and the navies of India and Egypt.

ABS continued applying its technical expertise to promote the protection of life and property leading to outspoken public support of stricter structural standards and tougher enforcement of existing standards. In particular, ABS publicly identified two conditions that had undermined public percep-

ABS maintained its lead in the offshore sector throughout the year, garnering classification contracts for some 200 offshore support vessels, tugs and barges in addition to a number of major deepwater development projects. ABS introduced its Vendor Coordination Program to smooth the worldwide flow of equipment into offshore energy projects, while producing several significant publications, including *Guidance Notes on Spectral-Based Fatigue Analysis for FPSO Systems* and the ABS *Guide for Crew Habitability on Offshore Installations*, the industry's first-ever classification standards addressing such human factors issues as noise, vibration, climate and lighting.

tions of classification – differing approaches among influential societies regarding minimally acceptable initial scantlings and the classification sector's traditional respect of shipowner's privacy regarding vessel information. ABS joined with collegial competitors, Lloyd's Register and Det Norske Veritas, to tackle the former by calling for common structural standards. With respect to the latter, ABS strongly supported an initiative to increase transparency of information and introduce a common scheme for identifying, targeting and monitoring vessels that may not be maintained to appropriate standards.

Now settled in at ABS Plaza in Houston, ABS undertook organizational change abroad to better serve its growing client base. Administration of the Southern Region of ABS Pacific was transferred from Singapore to Hong Kong and new management districts for West Africa, the Black Sea and the Caspian regions were established.

ABS CONSULTING CREATED

In 2001 ABS merged the skill sets of several affiliates into a new entity named ABS Consulting, which debuted as an integrated provider of wide-ranging risk management, structural engineering and management systems' consulting services. ≈

2002

INTEGRITY TRUMPS ADVERSITY

ABS' 140th year in operation was another year of challenge and change for the entire maritime industry, capped by the mid-November sinking of the ABS-classed tanker *PRESTIGE* off the northwest coast of Spain.

On passage in a winter North Atlantic storm, the *PRESTIGE* experienced rapid flooding of two empty ballast spaces. The captain called for help from Spanish rescue workers, expecting the vessel would be brought to a safe haven. Instead, local authorities forced the ship to steer away from the coast into the open North Atlantic. After six days of battering in heavy weather, the tanker broke in half and sank.

The European Union's response included moving to accelerate the ban on single-hull tankers by five years to 2010, pressing for greater regulation over tanker operations, and reaching for stricter oversight of classification societies.

As the classification society of record, ABS was thrust into the glare of intense media and political scrutiny. ABS was able to lead a vigorous defense of the role and responsibilities of class in the face of aggressive regulatory assault and adverse public perception of the maritime industry's safety record.

Despite the turbulence and an increasingly stringent regulatory environment, 2002 turned out to be ABS' busiest year to date. The gross tonnage of the ABS-classed fleet increased for the tenth straight year to 110.1 million gt, setting a company record for the second consecutive year. In particular, the enforced retirement of single-hull tankers under the new IMO MARPOL regulations sustained a strong ordering market across all sizes of that sector, with ABS winning a market-leading 29 percent of all tanker newbuildings. By year's end, 30 percent of all capesize bulk carriers on order were designated for ABS class as well.

In the energy industry, growing world interest in natural gas brought ABS a variety of gas transportation and storage projects, including classification of the first LNG tankers to be built in China – part of a larger involvement in China's Guangdong LNG import project.

ABS also contributed to developing LNG carrier technology, applying new sloshing analyses techniques within the SafeHull LNG application to a number of new carriers designed with the membrane containment system. And, using risk-based methodologies, ABS engineers developed new technical criteria for the design and installation of dual-fuel engines for the latest generation of LNG carriers.

ABS also supported alternative technologies to transporting liquefied gas, drafting its *Guidance Notes for Building and Classing Ships Carrying Compressed Natural Gas* (CNG). ABS worked closely with shipyards and designers to grant class "approval in principle" to several CNG vessel designs. ABS reached another gas energy landmark when selected as the classification society for the first newbuild floating production, storage and offloading (FPSO) unit for liquefied petroleum gas (LPG).

2002 also saw ABS strengthen its longstanding relationship with the US Military, as it began developing *Rules for Building and Classing Naval Vessels* following the Navy's decision to use adapted commercial vessel Rules in both its DD(X) destroyer and Littoral Combat Ship (LCS) programs. The Office of Naval Research contracted ABS to class its experimental aluminum X-Craft, and perform

plan review of another experimental catamaran made of composite materials.

The year was filled with futuristic projects, as the ABS Technology Department's vigorous research and development program ran some 70 research efforts in areas ranging from human factors engineering to ship structural performance. Among the most noteworthy were the start of two multi-year projects, one addressing the influence of hull deflection on shaft alignment problems, and another addressing the problem of parametric roll in containerships.

As its 140th year of service drew to a close, ABS began gearing up to add security issues to its traditional classification skills, drawing upon its ISM auditing experience to become an auditor under the new International Ship and Port Security Code adopted by the IMO. ≋

ABS took an active role as advisors to the US government delegation during the development of the International Ship and Port Facility Security (ISPS) Code.

Meanwhile, post-9/11 security concerns turned towards protection of LNG reception facilities, as governments began considering the use of floating terminals to limit civilian risk while handling an expected increased in world LNG transport. ABS responded with the industry's first *Guide for Building and Classing Offshore LNG Terminals.*

2003

LEADERSHIP IN AN EMBATTLED, EVOLVING INDUSTRY

The reverberations of the *PRESTIGE* incident continued to be felt in the maritime world throughout 2003, as the European Union considered further action against what it perceived to be an irresponsible maritime industry. IMO followed the EU lead and accelerated the single-hull tanker ban to 2010, while beginning a journey towards developing goal-based classification standards.

As in the previous year, an increasingly tough regulatory environment led to a busy and successful year for ABS, with an average of more than one new vessel per day coming into ABS class. For the third year running, ABS reached a record high gross tonnage in class, with the total climbing slightly to 110.6 million gt. For the first time in recent memory, the average age of the ABS fleet was less than 10 years.

The slow renewal of the world fleet accompanied a growing interest in such new concepts as life cycle management,

unified standards, safety equivalencies and risk and reliability – topics addressed by ABS' Technology Department in nearly 100 wide-ranging research and development projects.

2003 saw intense collaboration between ABS, Lloyd's Register and Det Norske Veritas in the Joint Tanker Project, an effort to develop common basic design criteria for tankers. A companion effort to develop common bulk carrier

Working with IACS, technical experts from ABS, LR and DNV formed the Joint Tanker Project to develop common structural design criteria for double hull oil tankers.

With more than 9 million gross tons of new vessels delivered to ABS class during the year, the team of new construction surveyors kept busy at shipyards in 40 countries around the globe.

Operators looking to take a rational risk-assessment approach to developing effective maintenance policies and practices found assistance in another new ABS publication, the *Guide for Survey Based on Reliability-Centered Maintenance*. The result of a three-year project, the new Guide offered guidance in effective planning and spending of maintenance budgets and focused on reducing system downtime through improved machinery reliability.

criteria among the other seven members of the International Association of Classification Societies (IACS) also began that year.

ABS produced three pioneering publications in 2003, addressing industry's growing interest in risk-based methodologies as an alternative to traditional, prescriptive Rules: the *Guide for Risk Evaluations for the Classification of Marine-Related Facilities*, the *Guidance Notes on Review and Approval of Novel Concepts*, and the *Guide for Surveys Using Risk-Based Inspection for the Offshore Industry*.

ABS also augmented its internal technologies in 2003, taking the latest step in its enhanced technology support program for survey activity. As part of the multi-year, multi-million dollar effort to increase administrative efficiency and support for field survey staff, ABS equipped its surveyors with portable computer-based virtual offices, loaded with applications to assist various aspects of survey preparation and reporting. From this moment forward, survey data could be entered into the ABS network directly by the surveyor, resulting in a dramatically shortened interval between completion of the survey and the moment full survey information became available to the owner or operator on the SafeNet network.

In an effort to improve the timeliness and quality of ABS design review services, an electronically based application was developed to simplify and expedite the plan review process.

ABS also addressed assisting the efficiency of its engineers. Spread across the world in 11 major shipping centers, ABS engineers provide immediate, personal service to both shipyards and owners. In 2003, ABS began a concentrated effort to develop an advanced, computer-based application that would revolutionize and accelerate the entire plan review process. Called Engineering 2000, the ambitious project proposed to make a wholly electronic process not only of the submission of drawings by the client but of the entire plan review process including filing, scheduling, control and technical project management.

In the offshore sector, two milestone agreements reflected the recognition by national authorities of ABS' technical capabilities. In the US, ABS signed a memorandum of agreement with the Minerals Management Service establishing a formal framework for scientific and technical collaboration in matters relating to offshore oil and gas operations. Across the world, the Azerbaijan State Mining Safety Committee announced its own technical collaboration with ABS regarding offshore oil and gas operations in the Azeri part of the Caspian Sea.

Facing exploration, drilling and production projects in record-breaking depths and harsh environments, offshore operators increasingly called on ABS for technical guidance in classing and certifying their solutions. ABS aided their efforts with an updated *Guide for Certification of Drilling Systems*, which supplemented traditional prescriptive Rules with a new option for a Safety Case or risk-based approach to certification.

For the maritime world, facing the fast-tracked implementation of the International Ship and Port Facility Security (ISPS) Code by July 2004, ABS issued its *Guide to Ship Security*, industry's first publication bringing together the latest IMO regulations and the relevant US Coast Guard requirements. ABS staff distributed thousands of copies at security seminars worldwide.

Meanwhile, ABS and the US Naval Sea Systems Command signed a landmark formal cooperative agreement on joint development of ABS *Rules for Building and Classing Naval Vessels*. For several years ABS and the US Navy had cooperated in a project to merge naval vessel requirements with commercial standards, to produce special Rules tailored to military use that would free Navy engineers to focus on the mission-related aspects of ship design. This new agreement brought ABS fully into the picture of supporting the design and acquisition of naval combatant ships. ≋

Representatives from ABS and the US Navy jointly developed the technical guidelines for the Naval Vessel Rules.

ROBERT D. SOMERVILLE

President: 1993-2004
Chairman: 2004-present

2004

LEADERSHIP CHANGES AS FLEET EXPANSION CONTINUES

ABS' new millennium evolution continued in 2004 with a changing of the guard in a number of key executive positions. In a carefully planned transition Chairman Frank Iarossi would retire in April and be replaced by President & CEO Robert Somerville, whose own duties as President would be assumed by ABS Americas President Robert Kramek.

The sustained expansion of the Chinese economy stimulated a rapid escalation in freight rates in 2004. Shipowner returns were boosted to heights not seen for decades and in turn funded a shipbuilding boom despite record-high steel prices.

This intense activity drove the size of the ABS-classed fleet to 114.4 million gt – the largest in the organization's history. Tanker contracts came at a rate of over one per day and again made ABS the world's premier tanker classification society, with 28 percent of all new orders in class. The growth in world trade in energy demand also led to a burst of class contracts for bulk

carriers and LNG tankers. By year's end more than half the in-service, ABS-classed fleet was 9 years of age or less.

2004 was also a year of technical milestones for ABS. A two-year project provided industry with the most comprehensive explanation of, and solutions for, the destructive phenomenon known as parametric roll to which containerships are

Relying on a fundamental physics theory, ABS researchers conducted numerical modeling and sequence simulations to illustrate the gravity force effects on ships as they roll, pitch and heave in a seaway.

particularly susceptible. A ship at sea rolls naturally but maintains control due to its intact stability. Under certain sea conditions, the rolling may quickly build to a level that

Members of the ABS LNG Carrier Project Team on a keel section under construction near team headquarters on Koje Island, Korea.

threatens the safety of the ship and can result in the loss of or damage to a large number of deck containers. ABS engineers developed criteria written into the *Guide for the Assessment of Parametric Roll Resonance in the Design of Container Carriers*, which allowed designers to screen designs for vulnerability to parametric roll and provided specific guidance to ships' crews on how to recognize and avoid the phenomenon.

ABS brought the energy sector some exciting initiatives as well, assembling a specialist survey team dedicated to gas carrier technology – the LNG Carrier Project Team – and developing the industry's first comprehensive training course in LNG technologies.

2004 was also a year of advanced LNG-related research projects focusing on such issues as fatigue life of the planned generation of very large LNG carriers of 200,000 cubic meters-plus capacities; the effects of sloshing within partially-filled membrane tanks; vibration from large, slow-speed diesel engines on membrane containment systems, in antici-pation of their future application to large LNG carriers; and effects related to propellers and propeller-induced vibration.

Stepping up involvement in gas technology issues, ABS became the first classification society accepted into associate

The US Navy's Littoral Combat Ship (LCS), a high-speed multi-mission platform ship, was designed and constructed to the technical guidelines in the ABS Naval Vessel Rules.

membership by SIGTTO, the Society of International Gas Tanker & Terminal Operators. Through SIGTTO and in cooperation with the International Association of Maritime Universities, ABS also announced a program to support the education and training of seafarers serving on LNG carriers.

ABS addressed the offshore industry's growing concerns over maintaining the structure of aging jackup drilling rigs by issuing a detailed Technical Commentary in its *Rules for Building and Classing Mobile Offshore Drilling Units* (MODUs). ABS also issued *Guidance Notes on Dynamic Analysis Procedures for*

Self-Elevating Drilling Units to more fully consider dynamic wave-induced loads on drilling units at the design stage.

In recognition of its distinctive achievements in energy technologies, ABS was appointed a spot on the National Petroleum Council, an oil and natural gas advisory committee to the US Secretary of Energy.

Meanwhile, the organization's relationship with the US Navy continued to grow with the completion of the ABS *Naval Vessel Rules.* The Rules were formally authorized by the newly formed ABS Naval Technical Committee and applied to the first US Navy combatants to be classed. As Navy requested ABS class for its next-generation submarine rescue system, ABS was asked to participate in the NATO working group on unified requirements for all submarine rescue systems worldwide to maximize interoperability of all navies using submarines.

2004 marked a significant milestone in the development of new common structural requirements for tankers over 150 meters in length with the release to industry for comment of the first draft of the proposed Rules.

This accompanied other advances in computational tool development. The Technology department advanced its program of building an intelligent database of all ABS Rules, Guides and relevant statutory requirements. Through enhancements to the Dynamic Load Approach and Spectral Fatigue Analysis programs, ABS became the first class society to include consideration of nonlinear sea loads within a structural response computer model of the full ship. ≋

ABS Technology and Information Management Systems worked closely to produce a user-friendly interface with shipyard designers.

2005

SERVICE BECOMES THE KEY DIFFERENTIATOR

World trade maintained its strongly positive growth throughout 2005 providing all sectors of the international shipping and offshore industries with an extended period of prosperity. This activity provided a buoyant business market for ABS.

In particular, newbuilding activity remained fevered. Despite warnings towards the end of the year that the rate of growth in world trade was declining, shipowners remained eager to place orders for ships for forward delivery through into 2009 at shipyards with already long orderbooks.

As could be expected, service delivery became a prime differentiator between class societies in such a demanding climate.

Engineering and survey staff remained busy as the ABS-classed fleet grew steadily to yet another new record of almost 121 million gross tons. This represented a remarkable 6.5 million gt increase in fleet size in just 12 months, reflecting the steady stream of deliveries from the shipyards, an influx of existing vessels switching to ABS class and an unusually low level of scrapping as owners sought to keep older tonnage working in the bull market.

Heightened new construction and repair activity kept the more than 800 ABS surveyors busy.

The many administrative efficiencies, particularly in the area of information systems, that ABS had introduced progressively over the previous five years provided the ability to absorb this increased level of activity while at the same time improving the speed and responsiveness of services to clients.

These IT projects had brought together the core functions of ABS – survey and engineering – and integrated them with the human resources and financial systems needed to fully support them in such a way as to provide unmatched service delivery.

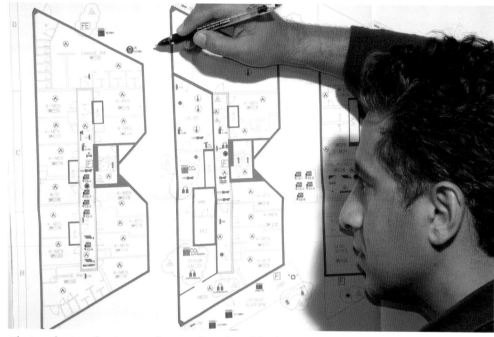

The introduction of an integrated system that allowed for filing, review and approval of drawings electronically marked a change in the way ABS engineers would approach their work.

In particular, the introduction of a sophisticated system that allowed for the electronic filing, review and approval of drawings marked a fundamental change in the way ABS engineers approached their work. On new projects, any of the 11 ABS engineering offices around the world could simultaneously access the drawings, the correspondence file and the entire review history related to a design. This flexibility meant that complex projects, particularly for the offshore sector, could

be handled more quickly and efficiently than before and in line with heightened client expectations.

The flexibility offered by the electronic systems support for engineering and survey was put to the test when, in August, a hurricane devastated New Orleans, home to 60 ABS employees working in the US Central District engineering and survey headquarters. Concern for the safety of the many ABS employees affected was the highest priority as many of

Hurricane Katrina's daylong rampage claimed lives and ravaged property in Louisiana, Mississippi and Alabama, where coastal areas remained under several feet of water. Katrina's storm surge caused several breaches in levees around New Orleans. Most of the city was subsequently flooded, as the breached drainage and navigation canals allowed water to flow from the lake into low areas of the city.

their homes were either destroyed or damaged. Fortunately no personal injuries were sustained.

As a result of the extensive, city-wide damage, the New Orleans office was closed for an extended period. The engineering staff moved to the Divisional headquarters in Houston and the survey staff immediately resumed operations either from their homes or from other ABS offices in the region. Clients received largely uninterrupted survey and

engineering services throughout despite the significant organizational disruptions that were experienced.

Other service related initiatives implemented during the year were the establishment of a new German National Committee, a new Middle East Technical Committee, the relocation of the ABS Europe Safety, Security and Environmental team to Piraeus from Dubai and a further significant expansion of the ABS staff in China, particularly in

Shanghai, to meet the demands of the rapidly expanding Chinese shipbuilding and repair industries.

The ABS Corporate Technology group was also reorganized into four new functional areas designed to give greater emphasis to client service. These consisted of Operational Safety and Evaluation; Research and Product Development; Engineering Support; and Rules and Standards Development. The technical expertise in each of these four areas was broadened.

Research was focused on issues that had been identified as being directly relevant to existing and future client needs as ABS sought to strengthen the traditional role of class, to improve service delivery and, where appropriate, to broaden the role of class to address safety issues beyond structural concerns and to incorporate new methodologies for evaluaing risk in the marine environment.

Perhaps no one sector benefited more from the ABS Corporate Technology expertise than the energy sector. Soaring prices for oil and gas fueled significant increases in oil company exploration budgets with deep water offshore plays at the forefront. Clients looked to ABS classification for technical guidance as the demand for energy pushed the boundaries of the exploration and production frontier. These demands allowed ABS to reinforce its position as the leading society providing services to the offshore sector based on its ability to advance sound technical solutions for projects and novel concepts that went beyond empirical experience. ≋

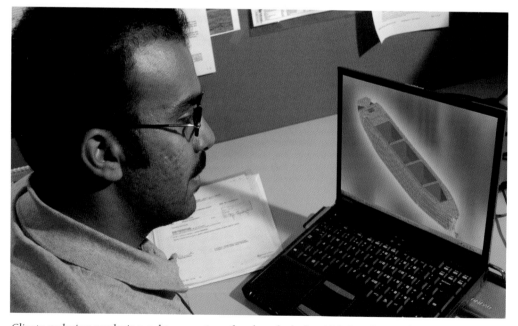

Clients exploring, producing and transporting oil and gas looked to ABS classification for technical guidance as the demand for energy pushed the boundaries of exploration and production.

APPENDICES

The first elected Board of Managers of the American Shipmasters' Association, 23 July 1862:

John D. Jones, President

Daniel Drake Smith

Elisha E. Morgan

Theo. B. Satterthwaite

Charles H. Marshall

Francis S. Lathrop

Robert L. Taylor

Richard Lathers

Ezra Nye

Alfred Edwards

William C. Thompson

Benjamin C. Morris

Moses H. Grinnell

C. Henry Koop

Leopold Bierwith

William H.H. Moore

Elwood Walter

Isaac H. Upton

Chairmen of the American Bureau of Shipping:

Stevenson Taylor	1926
J. Lewis Luckenbach	1950-1951
Walter L. Green	1952-1959
David P. Brown	1963-1964
Arthur R. Gatewood	1964
Andrew Neilson	1965-1971
Robert T. Young	1971-1979
William N. Johnston	1979-1987
Richard T. Soper	1987-1990
Frank J. Iarossi	1990-2004
Robert D. Somerville	2004-present

Presidents of the American Shipmasters Association and the American Bureau of Shipping:

John D. Jones	1862-1871
Theo B. Bleecker, Jr.	1871-1879
Horace J. Moody	1879-1881
John D. Jones	1881-1886
Theo B. Bleeker, Jr.	1886-1898
Anton A. Raven	1899-1916
Stevenson Taylor	1916-1926
Charles A. McAllister	1926-1932
J. Lewis Luckenbach	1933-1950
Walter L. Green	1950-1957
David P. Brown	1957-1963
Arthur R. Gatewood	1963-1964
Andrew Neilson	1964-1970
Robert T. Young	1970-1977
William N. Johnston	1977-1986
Richard T. Soper	1986-1990
Frank J. Iarossi	1990-1993
Robert D. Somerville	1993-2004
Robert E. Kramek	2004-present

The First Advisory Council of Scientific and Practical Experts in the Construction of Iron and Steel Vessels (aka the Advisory Council of Engineering and Marine Architects), 2 December 1892:

Robert Thurston, M.A., LL.D.,
Dr. Eng, Chairman

Commodore Theodore D. Wilson,
Chief Naval Constructor, US Navy

Commodore George W. Melville,
Engineer-in-Chief, US Navy

J. Harvard Biles, N.A., Instructor of Naval Architecture
and Marine Engineering, University of Glasgow

James E. Denton, M.E., Professor Experimental Mechanics,
Stevens Institute of Technology

William Gardner, N.A.

Lewis Nixon, N.A.

James S. Doran,
Superintendent Engineer

ABS: ITS ORGANIZATION AND ACTIVITIES

The American Bureau of Shipping is a not-for-profit organization. It has no capital stock and pays no dividends.

The income derived from its classification activity is generated from fees for its services. All funds are used solely for the performance of these services, and any surplus of receipts in any one year is used for the extension and improvement of such services, including research and development.

Management responsibilities are vested in the elected Board of Directors and the Council, chosen from the approximately 900 Members of ABS. This Membership is drawn from persons considered to be eminent within their marine field of endeavor, principally shipowners, shipbuilders, naval architects, marine engineers, engine builders, material manufacturers, marine underwriters and government representatives. None of the Members receive any compensation for services rendered.

As an international technical organization it is essential that ABS stays informed of and, when appropriate leads marine-related developments worldwide. ABS accomplishes this through a general committee structure consisting of individuals eminent in marine and offshore related industries.

Organized and managed in this manner, and reflective of the wide spectrum of interests of its Members, ABS provides the industry with a recognized organization for self-regulation.

Activity outside the realm of classification is conducted through the operating subsidiaries of ABS Group of Companies, Inc., an affiliate of ABS. These activities are conducted on a for-profit basis. Income is generated from fees for the products and services offered.

ABS CLASSIFICATION SERVICES

Nor can the classification society assume responsibility for managerial decisions of an owner or operator concerning crewing practices or operation of a classed vessel. It records, reports and recommends in accordance with what is seen at the time of a vessel's construction and subsequent surveys.

Through its classification survey procedure it is the intent of the society to prevent a vessel from falling into a substandard condition. If a vessel should be found to be in such a state, and the recommendations of ABS are not followed, then the society will suspend or cancel classification.

The responsibility of the classification society is to verify that merchant ships, marine and offshore structures presented to it comply with Rules that the society has established for design, construction, and periodic survey. Classification itself does not judge the economic viability of a vessel or structure. Neither is the society in a position to judge whether a vessel is ultimately employed according to the stated intended service for which it was classed.

CLASSIFICATION PROCEDURE

The primary means by which ABS pursues its mission is through classification of ships and other marine and offshore structures. Classification is a procedure involving:

- the development of standards, known as Rules
- technical plan review and design analysis
- surveys during construction and source inspection of materials, equipment and machinery
- acceptance by the Classification Committee
- subsequent periodic surveys for maintenance of class
- survey of damage, repairs and modifications

RULES AND STANDARDS DEVELOPMENT

Rules are derived from principles of naval architecture, marine engineering and kindred disciplines. A new Rule, or a proposed change to an existing Rule, originates with one of the ABS Technical Committees, from in-service experience, from IACS' recommendations or from the on-going research conducted by the technology staff at ABS. Research projects are conducted either directly by ABS or are undertaken jointly with industry, with academic and governmental organizations or other appropriate partners to best draw on the most qualified sources available.

After a design has been reviewed by ABS engineers, ABS field surveyors attend the vessel at the shipyard during the construction of the vessel. The surveyors verify that the approved plans are followed, good workmanship practices are applied, and the Rules are adhered to. During the construction of a vessel built to class, ABS surveyors witness, at the place of manufacture or fabrication, the tests of materials for the hull and certain items of machinery as required by the Rules. They also survey the building, installation and testing of the structural and principal mechanical and electrical systems.

Throughout construction ABS maintains an on-going dialogue with the owner and the builder to make sure the Rules are understood and adhered to, and to assist in resolving differences that may arise.

TECHNICAL PLAN REVIEW AND DESIGN ANALYSIS

When an owner first requests that the vessel or structure be classed, the shipyard or design agent presents drawings and calculations to ABS for a systematic detailed review for compliance with the Rules. ABS engineers review the plans to verify that the structural and mechanical details conform to the Rule requirements. Their review may also include sophisticated computer-based analytical procedures. In this way, ABS is able to determine whether the design is adequate in its structural and mechanical concept.

SOURCE INSPECTION OF MATERIALS, EQUIPMENT AND MACHINERY

For a vessel to meet ABS classification standards, the principal material and machinery must also meet ABS established standards, as confirmed by survey. Other components are required to meet the standards of the ABS Type Approval program which provides certification of marine equipment, materials and other products. ABS Type Approval certification is based on design review, prototype testing and annual surveys of the manufacturing facility. In the voluntary Type Approval Program, ABS certifies that enrolled manufacturers are capable of consistently producing a product in compliance with product specifications.

ABS is also recognized by many governments to approve life-saving, firefighting, fire protection, pollution prevention and control equipment on their behalf.

ACCEPTANCE INTO CLASS

When completed, a vessel undergoes sea trials attended by an ABS field surveyor to verify that the vessel performs according to Rule requirements. The vessel is then presented to the ABS Classification Committee which assesses the vessel's compliance with the *Rules* based on the collective experience of the Committee members and recommendations from the ABS staff. The Classification Committee is comprised of ABS Members drawn from the maritime industry, marine insurance, United States Coast Guard and ABS officers. When accepted by the Committee, formal certification is issued to the vessel. The vessel's classification information, characteristics and other particulars are then entered into the *ABS Record* – the registry of vessels classed by ABS.

SURVEYS AFTER CONSTRUCTION

ABS Rules require that every classed vessel be subject to periodic surveys of its hull and machinery to determine whether it is maintained in accordance with classification standards.

SURVEY OF DAMAGE, REPAIRS AND MODIFICATIONS

Should an ABS classed vessel sustain damage that may affect its classification status, the owner is required to inform the society. Upon request, ABS surveyors would then survey the vessel to determine whether the structure and machinery continue to meet the ABS Rules and, if not, verify that the repairs made return the vessel to a state of compliance with the Rules. Similarly, any structural modification of the vessel must be carried out in accordance with classification society requirements for the vessel to remain in class.

THE ESTABLISHMENT OF RULES

Rules are derived from principles of naval architecture, marine engineering, and other kindred disciplines. ABS develops and upgrades its Rules through a structure of special technical committees, and national and area technical committees. These committees permit ABS to maintain close contact with the numerous technological and scientific disciplines associated with the design, construction and maintenance of ships and other marine structures around the world.

GOVERNMENT AUTHORIZATIONS AND STATUTORY RESPONSIBILITIES

More than 100 governments have recognized the professional integrity and experience of ABS by authorizing the classification society to act as their statutory agent. These duties may include the conduct of surveys and the issuance of certificates in accordance with various international and national maritime Conventions and Codes, such as Load Line, Safety of Life at Sea (SOLAS), Tonnage and Marine Pollution (MARPOL).

These governments have recognized that ABS possesses a global network of exclusive, qualified surveyors and extensive resources in manpower and technology to conduct the technical reviews and surveys necessary to fulfill the various Convention requirements. Most governments do not have comparable resources or skills.

Through this long standing relationship with the maritime agencies of national governments, ABS has acquired extensive knowledge of national and international maritime regulations. It is able to draw on this knowledge in advising clients on how best to conform to these requirements, meet the documentary needs and accurately apply the criteria.

INTERNATIONAL CONVENTIONS AND STATUTORY CERTIFICATIONS

Although there are many International Conventions that apply to the shipping and offshore industries, four principal Conventions (and their subsequent amendments and/or protocols) have the most far reaching influence on the safety and environmental impact of these industries. They are the International Convention for the Safety of Life at Sea (SOLAS); the International Convention for the Prevention of Pollution from Ships (MARPOL); the International Tonnage Convention; and the International Convention on Load Lines.

As a Recognized Organization, ABS is authorized by many governments to perform technical reviews, inspect ships and marine structures, and issue certificates indicating compliance to these requirements.

SOLAS CERTIFICATES

ABS engineers and surveyors, working with industry and government representatives, can verify that the vessel is built and provided with the necessary equipment and features required by the SOLAS Convention.

Based on a satisfactory review and survey of the vessel, certificates can be issued indicating compliance with the requirements of the SOLAS regulation. These include:

- Safety Construction Certificate (SLC)
- Safety Equipment Certificate (SLE)
- Safety Radio Certificate (SLR)
- Passenger Ship Safety Certificate (SLP)

Where authorized by the flag State, document review and onshore and shipboard audits are also carried out by ABS

verifying that the safety management system complies with:

- International Management Code for the Safe Operation of Ships and for Pollution Prevention (ISM)

ABS also acts as a Recognized Security Organization by many governments, conducting security audits and verifying conformance with:

- International Ship and Port Facility Security Code (ISPS)

MARPOL CERTIFICATES

ABS will, upon request, perform review and survey relating to the issuance of the following MARPOL certificates:

- International Oil Pollution Prevention Certificate (IOPP)
- IMO Certificate of Fitness for Ships Carrying Liquefied Gases in Bulk (IGC)
- IMO Certificate of Fitness for Carriage of Dangerous Chemicals in Bulk (IBC)

LOAD LINE CERTIFICATES

A Load Line Certificate is issued on behalf of an Administration to indicate that a vessel is capable of carrying its intended cargo in a stable condition. The load line itself is a hull mark that indicates the maximum draft to which a vessel is permitted to safely load.

TONNAGE CERTIFICATES

In addition to the National or International Tonnage Certificates, Panama and Suez Canal Tonnage Certificates can be issued by ABS on behalf of those authorities. SOLAS and MARPOL regulations specify arrangements and equipment requirements based on the ship's admeasured tonnage.